KU-035-256

CONTENTS

Leisure and Tourism GNVQ: Intermediate Textbook

Leisure and Tourism GNVQ: Intermediate Textbook

Brian Jones   Jill Kennaugh   Christine Parry   Peter Trigg

Series editor: Peter Trigg

Butterworth-Heinemann Ltd
Linacre House, Jordan Hill, Oxford OX2 8DP

 A member of the Reed Elsevier plc group

OXFORD   LONDON   BOSTON
MUNICH   NEW DELHI   SINGAPORE   SYDNEY
TOKYO   TORONTO   WELLINGTON

First published 1995

British Library Cataloguing in Publication Data
A catalogue record for this book is available
from the British Library

ISBN 0 7506 2157 5

Composition by Genesis Typesetting, Laser Quay, Rochester, Kent
Printed in Great Britain by
Martins The Printers Ltd, Berwick upon Tweed

CONTRIBUTORS

Series Editor
Peter Trigg, Head of School, Wirral
Metropolitan College; BTEC Adviser and Lead
External Verifier for Leisure and Tourism

Contributors
Brian Jones, Lecturer, Wirral Metropolitan
College

Chris Parry, Lecturer, Wirral Metropolitan
College

Jill Kennaugh, Lecturer, Wirral Metropolitan
College

ACKNOWLEDGEMENTS

British Airways
Butlins Holiday Worlds
Catalyst Museum Widnes, Cheshire
Cheshire County Council (Divided Loyalties Project)
Chester Leisure Centre – Chester County Council
Christopher Pashley – Consultant
English Heritage
English Tourist Board
Granada Studios Tour plc.
Hoylake and West Kirby News
Janet Morris (Princes Trust Volunteers)
Leisure Opportunities Journal (Dicestar Ltd)
Martin & Mason – Leisure Consultants
National Trust
Thomas Cook Travel Agents

EVIDENCE COLLECTION

The elements and performance criteria that each task will help you collect evidence for are listed below each task.

Please note that within Unit 3 some tasks are purely for awareness raising rather than covering specific elements and performance criteria.

INVESTIGATING LEISURE AND TOURISM

Introduction

The leisure and tourism industry is one of the fastest growing areas in the British and world economies. The advent of better conditions for people in work coupled with advances in transportation and connection routes and motorways has opened up a truly worldwide opportunity for travel and the acquisition of new leisure and cultural activities. It is important that we appreciate how and why these developments have taken place. It is not our intention to give a history lesson about travel and tourism but we will attempt to show you some of the important milestones that have led to the present situation.

The Roman Empire was a very civilized culture with many of its people educated and skilled; these assets were put to very good use in their campaigns throughout Europe, including the British Isles. The Romans built roadways with a purpose, which along their length would allow for stopping places with fresh water and accommodation for their soldiers and engineers. Today in Britain there can be found remains of the Roman fortress towns such as Chester, Colchester, York and many others. The Romans left a legacy of good roads, charted country via maps and a strong communications network. This was the bedrock for the future travellers and traders in the early middle ages.

Travel in its earliest form was due to religious activities whereby priests, monks and, even earlier, apostles would take to the road either by horse or donkey (or a combination of the two) and a cart in order to spread the word of God to people in towns and cities. This activity was a way of informing the people and would take up most if not all of their lives in a travelling capacity. During this time they would meet people from many different backgrounds, beliefs and cultures, they would talk of these people in their travels and occasionally would

inspire others who could afford it and also had the means of transport to visit such places.

However, we must remember that travel was not all for positive reasons. Religious aspects included 'spreading the word', visiting shrines and holy sites and also included holy wars such as the Crusades.

In our own history this invoked King Richard to travel with many soldiers to the Holy Land for battle with Arabs to save Jerusalem. Soldiers that did manage to return to Britain told of many hardships but also of the very different culture and architecture of the areas where they fought. These sites have now become tourist attractions in Israel.

Religion continued to be a prime source for travel and travellers, but as advances in methods of travel were achieved, such as sailing ships in the fifteenth century, a new type of travel was emerging. The explorers and new traders of the world were literally beginning to discover new worlds. New commodities such as tobacco, potatoes, spices and plants were being bought back to Britain, Spain, Portugal and the Netherlands, who at the time were the prime movers in trading and exploration.

Tales of exciting new lands with people of very different cultures were being told in the courtyards of the nobility and the wealthy, encouraging a few to explore likewise, while the wealthy who remained set up the shipping companies for the sale of the goods that returned and great profits were made. Religion still played an important part, however, and missionaries would travel in the trading ships to the continents of Africa, America and India to spread Christianity. Little pockets of England started to grow throughout the world, e.g. Raffles Hotel in Singapore, and eventually created their own travel market for relatives to visit them.

The expansion of trade continued to grow but there was a need to reduce the travelling time because competition was increasing amongst trading companies. The 'Tea Clippers' war was a

testimony to that, but the *Cutty Sark* and her equals were no match for what was to come, the Age of Steam. The early seventeenth century saw a revolution in the advancement of transportation by way of the steamship and the steam train. Travel, apart from being quicker, was getting slightly more comfortable and also more affordable by the new wealthy, which in turn created a travel market based on leisure.

It was very fashionable to visit areas of great artistic interest such as Greece, Italy and France. Travel, however, was totally reliant on the skill of the traveller and how good they were with foreign languages. There was little in the way of printed timetables and schedules: it was very much a question of 'who dares wins'. This was the situation until 1847 when a young Methodist by the name of Thomas Cook organized an excursion by rail to a temperance meeting, from Leicester to Loughborough. The party included people from all over Britain and was such a success that the meeting's organizers asked him to repeat the exercise.

Figure 1.1 The *Cutty Sark*

Figure 1.2

This natural talent of Thomas Cook continued to flow and the young man staged more complicated excursions involving train, boat and accommodation in hotels for his customers. This organization took a lot of worry out of the travel for his passengers so his fame quickly spread, to the extent that in 1851 Prince Albert asked Cook to organize the travel arrangements for the Great Exhibition which took place in Hyde Park in London. Over 160,000 people were transported via the Cook firm, which included organizing accommodation in hotels, guest houses and dormitories. This testing event made Thomas Cook virtually a household name amongst the wealthy and, probably for the first time, the not so rich.

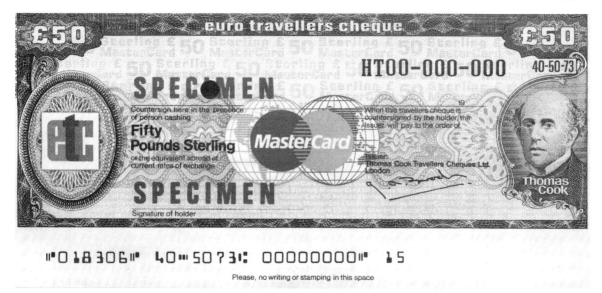

Figure 1.3

Thomas Cook with his son John moved from strength to strength with excursions to Europe including Paris, Geneva and, a particular favourite of the British, the Swiss Alps. From there Asia and Africa were on the itinerary with a network of agents' offices (Thomas Cook of course!) throughout the world. The Cook family continued with their innovations and produced full itineraries (a detailed route of travel arrangements) for passengers, including currency. Cook's name was so good that hoteliers around the world would accept his name on a voucher supplied by the guest which would then be redeemed for cash at Cook's offices. This saved the traveller from needing to carry large sums of cash, in effect the first traveller's cheque (a traveller's cheque is for a fixed amount that may be cashed on signature, usually internationally).

The Cook family did much to improve the prospect of travel for many people. There were, however, other travel operators who were operating at approximately the same time as Thomas Cook: Sir Henry Lunn, who formed Lunn Poly; Dean and Dawson, which started in 1871 as the Polytechnic Touring Association; and Frames Tours, established in 1881. Across the Atlantic in America, Henry Wells and William Fargo, later to become Wells Fargo, were spreading their stagecoach network across the western states of America. It is true to say, however, that Wells Fargo's involvement in tourism and travel did not begin until the early twentieth century, though their distribution network for mail and banking material formed the base of the major travel routes between towns and cities.

The early twentieth century saw an increase in travel and tourism due to a more stable travel network, coupled with better healthcare in Central Europe which made the prospect of illness whilst abroad less of a daunting prospect. At this time early forms of travel insurance (travel insurance is purchased to cover the traveller against any personal mishap whilst travelling, e.g. accident to the person, loss of money, ill health) were emerging too.

The outbreak of the First World War did slow travel and tourism down but in a strange way assisted further tourism after it. The outbreak of war brought about more control of people moving between different countries and it was for this reason that passports were introduced. Prior to this British people did not require one for travel in Europe. But the whole process left the structure for travel after the war in place with European paperwork replaced by a single document, the passport (a passport is an official document issued by a government certifying

EUROPEAN COMMUNITY

UNITED KINGDOM OF
GREAT BRITAIN
AND NORTHERN IRELAND

PASSPORT

Figure 1.4

the holder's identity and citizenship, and entitling the holder to travel under its protection to and from foreign countries).

Like the crusaders, the returning soldiers had travelled extensively in their area of battle and brought home tales of drudgery but also of the interest of the regions they visited. Soldiers with family and friends would revisit these areas in peacetime (e.g. the D-day celebrations during 1994).

The period between the First and Second World Wars saw an increase in both domestic and European holidays. However, the Great Depression in the early 1930s did curtail the European market for a number of years as unemployment was high and also only the strongest businesses survived, which left previously wealthy businessmen in a state of poverty. Domestic holidays, however, flourished with the traditional resort towns of Brighton, Scarborough and Blackpool seeing new competition from Llandudno, Skegness, Clacton and Colwyn Bay. Many of the annual tourists were dependent on the railways for their travel to the resorts but the advent of the factory-produced motor car was about to turn the transportation market on its head and would have done so sooner if not for the outbreak of the Second World War.

The war years saw travel mainly for mobilizing troops and the transportation of government officials and journalists covering the war campaigns. Those civilians that did travel stayed well away from the European and transatlantic routes as the German Navy was conducting its U-boat campaign against civilian and military ships. Travel by air was seen as a safer alternative, particularly in America, and expansion of their domestic routes was continued as not a single bomb dropped on the United States due to its distance from the European mainland. Military expansion with new aeroplanes for bombing and troop movements was also being developed in Great Britain and it was this innovation that was going to change transportation in the post-war years.

After the Second World War, there was a need to rebuild great areas of the United Kingdom and mainland Europe, due to the destruction caused by battle and bombing by the Allies and German forces. This period created work and prosperity for a great number of people: manufacturing companies expanded and building and engineering companies grew. In general the period of the late 1950s and in particular the 1960s saw the average household with more disposable income (disposable income is the part of our income that we are free to spend on non-essentials after we have paid all our important or essential bills, e.g. money we might spend on going on holiday) due to full employment, better working conditions and, above all, pay. The trade unions introduced 'collective bargaining' (bargaining between employers and employees over wages, terms of employment, etc., when the employees are represented by a trade union or some other collective body) which meant workers did not have to negotiate individually. The trade union negotiated for all its members who collectively had great bargaining power, which in turn led to large increases in pay for the workers.

This increased wealth was directed in several directions, principally:

- House purchase
- Motor car purchase
- Individual holidays
- Expenditure on leisure activities, e.g. golf, cinema visits, records (there were no tapes or CDs at that time) and drinking.

People's prosperity created the demand for better and more innovative (bringing in new methods and ideas, making changes) travel and holiday products. As mentioned earlier, the factories that produced the motor car were going to change the transportation of individuals. Dependence on the railways was about to decrease. Individual wealth saw the average household purchasing their own car and with it greater freedom to travel where they wished.

There was also one other factor which turned the holiday market into the one we know today, and that was air travel. The end of the war saw great stockpiles of aircraft which had been previously used for military purposes. Military pilots were now in a peacetime economy and were able to put their experience to great use. A few brave men and women

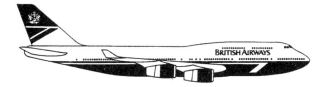

Figure 1.5

purchased the aircraft and started the early charter airlines for domestic and European travel. Among them were Harold Bamberg and Freddie Laker, who are recognized as the forefathers of the charter flight.

Development in air transport continued with better engines and more comfort for transatlantic, European and Eastern travellers. There was competition taking place with more innovative methods being sought. Tour operators up until the 1950s tended to book a block of seats on scheduled flights – the first booking of a whole plane was not undertaken until Vladimir Raitz of Horizon Holidays organized a 'pilot' package holiday. He chartered a complete aircraft for 300 passengers and committed his company to filling it. His gamble paid off and he even managed to reduce the costs to the passengers. Over the next few years Raitz continued to develop these activities.

Arrangements for a package holiday are handled by a tour operator, who books hotel accommodation and makes all the necessary flight arrangements. The holidaymaker just has to arrive at, say, the airport and then the tour operator takes over, transporting the holidaymaker to and from his or her airport to their holiday resort.

Other tour operators also saw the benefits and mirrored Horizon Holidays' initiative, with more operators competing in the package market. This competition saw expansion of holidays being offered in Spain, Greece, Italy, Portugal and Switzerland for winter holidays. The concept of mass tourism was now well under way. On the domestic holiday scene there was the development and expansion of holiday camps (a camp for holidaymakers with accommodation, entertainment, and facilities on site) throughout the UK (previously introduced by Billy Butlin at Skegness in 1936). This market included the now household names of Pontins and Warners. The holiday camp holiday became the staple diet of the British holidaymaker between 1936 and 1970, but the expansion and reduction of prices of the European package holiday, coupled with the uncertain British weather, has since led to its demise.

The population boom in the 1960s saw by the mid-1970s young people wanting a different type of holiday altogether. Their expectations were based on the very attraction and appeal of the European 'fun in the sun' holiday advertised by the tour operators and pressure was applied by them on parents; four years later they were going on their own. The rest is history!

In the previous pages we have looked at a 'snapshot' of how travel and tourism, coupled with leisure pursuits, has developed over the last century. There are, however, a number of activites which we have not looked at, but will discuss in later sections. These are:

- Camping and caravan holidays
- Theme parks
- Activity holidays
- Weekend breaks
- Leisure parks
- Holiday worlds and centres

Figure 1.6 Starcoast World, a Butlin's holiday resort

Task 1.1

In the previous pages we have discussed how leisure and travel tourism has developed over the last century. We mentioned Sir Henry Lunn of Lunn Poly fame. As part of your investigation, prior to reading the next unit, visit your nearest branch of Lunn Poly, or write to their head office, for a brief history of how the company was developed and how it has changed since it first commenced business.
Element 1.1, PC3 and 6

Definition of leisure and tourism

When one is asked to define leisure and tourism it is very difficult to give a simple answer as up to 15 years ago they were considered different industries and were very segmented. In more recent times the close relationship between the two has been recognized; indeed, the very name of your course is titled Leisure and Tourism and is made up of two courses which were previously run separately.

In preparation for evidence for your portfolio, the following definitions may be useful.

Leisure

Leisure is generally considered to be the time remaining after work, travel to and from work, sleep and other necessary household tasks. This is time known as 'discretionary time' or in other words time which you can choose to use as you wish. This could include travel, sporting activities, arts, entertainment and study, etc.

The leisure industry

The leisure industry, however, is made up of organizations, firms and establishments with a common function of providing goods and services for use in leisure time. In many terms the industry serves the leisure market and attracts people to spend their disposable income (money left after all necessary payments, such as rent, mortgage commitments, etc.).

The leisure industry presently represents a large proportion of people's expenditure, as may be seen in some of the tables and illustrations in later sections of this book.

Tourism

In very simple terms tourism means 'tourist travel'. The term is used to describe the various parts of the tourist industry such as:

● Travel
● Accommodation
● Retail
● The tourist.

Types of facilities, products and services

Accommodation

The type of accommodation in the local area depends on the geographic location, such as town, village, resort or city, as well as amenities and attractions, e.g. theme parks, arenas,

concert stadiums or conference centres, which attract differing types of people with differing requirements. Depending on the type of accommodation the product or services will vary.

For example, a guest house will provide a room, bathroom and communal lounge and the service will include meals, depending on what tariff you are requiring: Bed and Breakfast, Bed and Breakfast and Evening meal, or Full Board.

A hotel, however, may be able to provide a bedroom, bathroom *en suite* with shower or jacuzzi, TV in your room, telephone, trouser press and tea/coffee-making facilities. The types of service offered will vary according to the size and category of hotel but could include:

● Room service for meals
● Dining room
● Coffee shop
● Leisure suite
● Function room
● Conference centre
● Secretarial services.

The provision offered will vary in price and will depend further on whether the services requirement is weekday or weekend. Hotels often sell weekend breaks for tourists which are cheaper than the normal business rate during the week. Leisure facilities in hotels may be available to non-residents; this helps to keep costs down over the year.

Accommodation is often governed by local amenities (pleasant or useful features in a locality) and attractions for that area – these will dictate the range and size of provision. For specific services and pursuits, a hotel guide is the best way to establish the range in your area. Guides are published by the Tourist Information office (office that provides tourist information for visitors, e.g. details of local hotels, guest houses, theatres, cinemas, restaurants, etc.) locally, as well as the motoring organizations, such as the AA and the RAC.

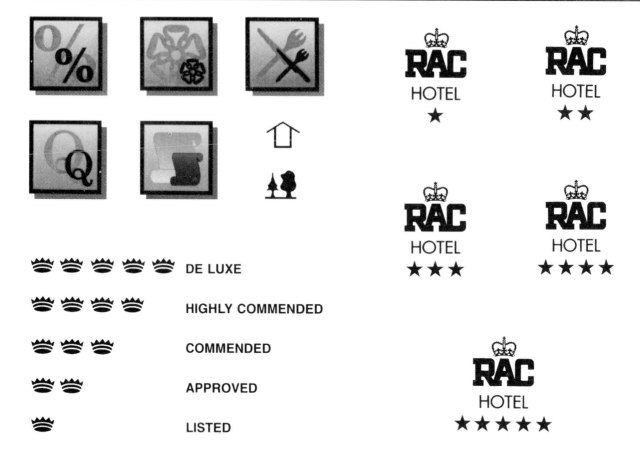

DE LUXE

HIGHLY COMMENDED

COMMENDED

APPROVED

LISTED

Figure 1.7

Catering and hospitality

A wide range of products and services may be offered under this heading, but once again location, attractions and amenities will dictate the amount and type of provisions. The main types of catering services offered will normally include:

- *Pubs* – offering food, such as Beefeaters, Harvesters and Brewers Fayre
- *Restaurants* – French, Bistro and Italian
- *Ethnic restaurants* – Indian, Chinese and Mexican
- *Fast food* – McDonald's, Burger King, Kentucky Fried Chicken and Wimpy
- *Speciality restaurants* – Tandoori, Hamal and vegetarian.

Entertainment

This will often start with the provision of food and drink in various ways from cabaret and dance clubs to nightclubs with restaurants. Popular venues such as discos will offer food, but choice is often limited. The licensing laws state that drink may only be offered after normal hours where food is being provided and that is what the disco is really out to achieve.

Theatres too will offer some form of food and drink provision by way of coffee shop, bistro or theatre bar. A very popular event in theatres now is to offer a combined dinner and theatre ticket – this happens more in city theatres than in towns or urban areas and is linked with a specific hotel or restaurant near to the theatre. The package includes your first and main courses served, then a break to attend the theatre performance and then back to the hotel to conclude your evening with dessert and coffee. This package benefits both the theatre and the hotel or restaurant as they will both promote each other by providing adverts in the theatre about the hotel and in the restaurant which promote the theatre and its attractions.

Education

This area does not immediately spring to mind as a leisure pursuit, but for many it is, as well as being a method of improving oneself. There is

therefore a real opportunity for educational establishments to create leisure markets.

Educational establishments such as colleges and universities which have accommodation on their campuses can offer a range of activities that include sport and recreation, events, short courses, conferences, exhibitions and many more whilst at the same time offering accommodation, meals and services for customers who are attending from out of the area (accommodation is normally only provided in the holiday periods as students would be housed in it during term times). Many tour companies are now using university campuses as accommodation venues: this collaboration suits both parties as it provides a change from alternatives like hotels while raising money for universities and colleges.

Figure 1.8 A university campus

Task 1.2

Find out what your local university offers for holiday courses and accommodation for visitors.

Element 1.1, PC3 and 6

There are two areas where the product and services offered will depend on its natural resources, geographical location and ability to market its products. They are:

● Travel and tourism
● Sport and recreation.

Travel and tourism

Tourism can be divided into business tourism and leisure tourism.

Business tourism

Business tourism is dependent on its facilities being offered, such as:

● Exhibition halls
● Conference centres
● Accommodation
● Infrastructure.

Areas which focus on business tourism are London, Birmingham, Glasgow and Manchester. These locations are served with good travel links by road, rail and air, have good exhibition arenas and are well equipped with accommodation providing a range of facilities.

Their function is not exclusive, however, and we see leisure and tourism equally in the same locale but for different reasons such as events, concerts, sports and leisure activities.

Leisure tourism

Leisure and tourism may be a product of an area's natural beauty such as the Lake District or North Wales, its cultural interest such as Salisbury and Stonehenge, or its historical interest such as York or Chester.

Figure 1.9 Stonehenge

It may also be a combination of the above, such as London which includes the seat of the monarchy plus a tremendous range of historical and cultural interests for the tourist. Leisure and tourism may also be busiest in activities such as the areas in proximity to a racecourse, motor racing circuit, water sports location or natural phenomenon such as snow in the case of Aviemore in Scotland. One thing in common for all the above is the area's ability to promote itself locally and nationally and in some cases internationally. This promotion may be undertaken by the tourist boards and information centres of the local council. Advertising and promotion materials (gradual development from a simple to a more complex process of advertising) will be dealt with in later sections.

Sport and recreation

The role of sport and recreation within the leisure and tourism industry is crucial. It is a major provider for both local and national business. It is a provider for businesses in:

● Media
● Transportation
● Accommodation
● Dining
● Sundries (pendants, flags, bags and umbrellas)
● Clothing (football, rugby, team strips)
● Sporting venues (swimming pools, football and rugby grounds, sports centres, arenas, fairgrounds and racing circuits).

Task 1.3

Visit your local Football League club and shop to establish the range of products they sell to promote the club. Try to find out the number of suppliers who produce those goods for the club and what is the approximate value of the goods.

Element 1.2, PC2

All of the above, plus many more, employ a large number of people in direct and indirect services within sport, sporting activities and recreation. The type of business and the type of activity will depend on the quantity and size of venue available. This will often indicate where a major sporting event will take place, such as:

● FA Cup Final
● Commonwealth Games
● World Student Games
● The Grand National

The above examples are staged according to a mixture of tradition, size and investment. Let us look more closely at each.

The FA Cup Final

A premier event with two football clubs playing for a major trophy. Arguably, if only the teams' supporters attended, the game could be played in one of the larger premier division club grounds. But the interest value is much greater, so that is why Wembley Stadium in London is used. It has the capacity to seat over 80,000 people, plus private boxes for corporate hospitality, and has good parking, catering and travel facilities.

The Grand National

This is the world's greatest steeplechase, held at Aintree race course in Liverpool. Tradition plays a part here, but also only a few race courses can stage a four-mile race with only two circuits of the course. But above all, the character and history of the race and its notorious fences would be lost elsewhere. Aintree is known throughout the world. To stage it elsewhere would mean rebuilding the name and venue, which could affect the millions of pounds in revenue from television and sponsors.

Commonwealth Games – Edinburgh 1986
World Student Games – Sheffield 1992

Both of these events were a result of successful bids to the respective federations (a group of those people or governing bodies interested in the sport, in this case the Commonwealth and World Student Games) to stage the events which are by nature moved around various venues throughout the world (similar to the Olympic Games). They required a lot of investment in existing facilities by upgrading them and new building of others, coupled with improved travel and communications links as well as accommodation for participants and visitors.

This required obtaining funding for both public and commercial sectors as well as the local councils. Sadly both events proved costly and were not supported as well as hoped, but the venues are now used for other prestigious events on a national and international level as well as providing an excellent facility for the local residents. So in the long run the investment made will be returned and the reputation of both areas can trade on the experience of hosting such events.

As you can see, sport and recreation can play a major role in the local and national economies, but can also present benefits and problems for the local community. We will investigate this further in the next section.

Case study

The government has been keen to regenerate areas in the north of the UK which were hit particularly badly when manufacturing saw great losses of jobs. Manchester has done much to help itself and create employment for its people, the Olympic Games bid being one such initiative.

Manchester has bid twice to stage the Olympic Games. Its first bid was for 1996 and the second for the year 2000. In its first bid to the IOC (The International Olympic Committee) it failed as it was thought that the necessary changes to the surrounding area could not be achieved in the time available (approximately 4 years).

These changes would have included new roads to improve motorway links, new stadiums to stage the track and field events and improvements in sporting facilities in the surrounding area, such as Chester and Liverpool. Both cities were listed as providing some of the venues for events such as rowing and cycling.

Manchester did extremely well in putting together a package which included public and private investment. However, as we all now know, it failed and Atlanta in America won the bid to stage the 1996 Olympic Games. Manchester was not disenchanted, however, and under their chairman, Sir Bob Scott, a second bid was put forward for the year 2000. The period 1990–1994 saw great changes in Manchester and the surrounding area with a continuation of the planning laid down for the 1996 bid but also further money being spent on:

- A second airport terminal
- New and improved road communications
- A velodrome (for cycling competitions)
- Improvements in local transport – such as the new tram system in Manchester
- Investment in new hotels
- Purpose-built accommodation for the prospective athletes
- Landscaping of the M6 corridor to improve facilities for tourists and other visitors.

During the period leading up to the bid for the Games in the year 2000, Manchester promoted itself throughout the world and indeed had the support of world figures such as Sir Bobby Charlton, Princess Anne (who is a member of the IOC), Chris Boardman (Olympic medallist for cycling in 1992) and many more.

The government supported the bid with £50 million to build the velodrome stadium. This was an exciting period for Manchester and a lot of improvements and additional facilities were created. As we know, history repeated itself and the second bid failed and the Games will be staged in Sydney, Australia.

Despite this and all the problems created for local people by way of the extensive building, Manchester now has a place in the scheme of world events. It is internationally known and provides a range of major sporting facilities as well as excellent facilities for the tourist with travel links throughout the world via its new airport terminal. These facilities will no doubt be used for national and international events, thus increasing the number of visitors, competitions and tourists to the area.

Facilities available locally and nationally

This section looks at the different areas of leisure and tourism which you would find in towns and cities up and down the country. It also looks at the typical facilities you would expect to find and discusses their impact on the local and national community in terms of economy and the relationship with the various parties who provide leisure and tourism activities.

What you need to know

When looking at the leisure and tourism scene in your local area it is important to establish under which sector the provision falls:

- *Public* – run with the assistance of local ratepayers' money
- *Private* – privately owned with possible assistance from bank loans
- *Voluntary* – run for the community and dependent on donations from people or through money-raising activities.

The local leisure scene

Much of the leisure provision in your local area has been established for many years, such as:

- Parks
- Leisure centres

- Libraries
- Museums
- Art galleries
- Football clubs
- Cinemas
- Dance halls
- Nightclubs
- Theatres

There are also likely to be hobby or interest activities such as the Girl Guides, Brownies, Cubs or Scouts.

Task 1.4

List the above examples under the headings: public, private and voluntary sector. On completion of the list you will probably find that an even spread covers all three sectors.
Element 1.1, PC3
Element 1.2, PC2 and 3

Task 1.5

Look once again at your list and reorganize under indoor and outdoor venues. How many are a mix of both?
Element 1.2, PC1
Element 1.1, PC3

You will probably find the larger amount falls under indoor activities. Although traditionally the UK was involved in outdoor activities as leisure pursuits, our weather and climate are not suited to all the normal activities so there is a tendency for 'activity' sports such as tennis and badminton to fall off during the winter season.

It was only as recently as 1964 that the leisure centre as we know it was established. This facility enabled people to pursue the typically

THERE'S SOMETHING FOR EVERYONE!

SWIMMING

LEISURE POOL

School Holidays	Weekdays	10.00am-9.30pm
Public Swimming	Mon - Fri	12.00-9.30pm
Public Swimming	Sat & Sun	10.00-5.00pm
Adult Only Swim	Monday	7.30-9.30pm
Families Only Swim	Friday	6.00-7.30pm
Early Morning Dip	Mon - Fri	7.15-8.30am
	Saturday	8.15-9.45am
Lunchtime Swim (T. Pool)	Mon - Fri	12.30-2.00pm
Water Fun	Mon - Fri	12.00-9.30pm
Free Slides	ALL WEEK	

SWIMMING

PROGRAMMES

Aqua Natal	Monday	10.00-11.00am
Aqua Aerobics	Monday	11.15-12.15pm
	Wednesday	10.00-11.00am
		6.00-7.00pm
		8.30-9.30pm
Adult Swim Lessons		
Tues, Wed & Thurs (course)		11.30-12.30pm
Friday (casual)		11.30-12.30pm
Late Night Swims (Training Pool)	Mon	9.30-10.30pm
Ladies Only	Tuesday	9.30-10.30pm
Mixed Adults	Monday	9.30-10.30pm
Mixed Adults	Wednesday	9.30-10.30pm

NEW!

Introducing our all new fitness suite incorporating Cardio-Vascular equipment such as computer rowers, steppers and bikes as well as resistance modules. Most facilities may be used by wheelchair athletes.

fitness 2000

AEROBICS

Mon	6.00-7.00pm	Proj Hall	HIGH IMPACT
	7.00-8.00pm	Main Hall	NORMAL LEVEL
Tues	6.00-7.00pm	Main Hall	NORMAL LEVEL
Wed	11.00-12.00pm	Act Hall	WHOLE WORKOUT
	7.00-8.00pm	Main Hall	NORMAL LEVEL
Thurs	6.00-7.00pm	Act Hall	NORMAL LEVEL
	7.00-8.00pm	Main Hall	WHOLE WORKOUT
Fri	6.00-7.00pm	Act Hall	HIGH IMPACT
	7.00-8.00pm	Main Hall	NORMAL LEVEL
Sun	10.30-11.30am	Main Hall	WHOLE BODY

STEP AEROBICS

Tue, Fri, Sat & Sun	10.00-11.00am
Monday & Friday & Sun	7.00-8.00pm
Tues, Wed & Thurs	6.00-7.00pm
STEP AND TONE (Bums, Tums and Thighs)	Thursday 9.45 - 11.00am

KEEP FIT

FITNESS SUM

Mixed Fitness Weights	Mon	7.00-8.00pm
Mixed Fitness Weights	Wed	7.00-8.00pm
Ladies Only	Thurs	7.00-8.00pm
Ladies Shape Up	Wed	10.00-11.00pm
Circuit Training	Wed	7.00-8.00pm
Weight Induction Classes	Mon	6.00-7.00pm
Yoga	Mon	8.30-10.00am
	Tues	8.15-9.45pm
	Thurs	11.00-12.30
Fifty Plus	Mon, Tues & Thurs	2.00-4.00pm
Badminton, Swimming, Table Tennis and Coaght		
Lunchtime Package	Tues & Thurs	11.00 Onwards
Popmobility, Sauna & Swimming		
Callisetics	Mon	10.00-11.00am Act Hall
Ladies Recreation	Wed	9.30-12.00pm
Badminton, Squash and Swimming		

SAUNA SUITE

Male - Mon, Wed & Fri		12.00-10.30pm
Female - Tues & Thurs		12.00-10.30pm
Mixed - Saturday		10.00-1.30pm
Sundays		10.00-5.30pm
Couples Only-Saturday		1.30-5.30pm
Sunbeds		
Male - Mon, Wed & Fri		12.00-9.30pm
Saturday		12.00-4.30pm
Sunday		12.00-4.30pm
Female - Mon - Fri		12.00-10.00pm
Sat & Sun		12.00-4.30pm

AROMATHERAPY BY APPOINTMENT

PLUS

OPENING TIMES: MON - SAT 7.15am - 11pm DAILY. SUN 10am-11pm

Swimming: Peak rates apply after 5pm Monday to Friday, also 10am - 5pm Saturday, Sunday & during school holidays.

Leisure Pool is open at 12noon and 10am during school holidays.

Other clubs/activities include - Life Saving - Canoeing - Swimming School - Trampolini (Disabled) - Toddlers Gymnastics - Mums & Tots Swim - Badminton - Naturist Swim - Archery - 50 Plus Table Tennis - Climbing - Juggling - Netball, as well as a comprehensive range of 10 Martial Arts Clubs.

Dry Sports: Peak rates apply after 5pm Monday to Friday, and 10am-6pm Saturday and Sunday.

Concessionary and off-peak prices apply BEFORE 5pm weekdays only. NOT WEEKENDS and HOLIDAYS.

A comprehensive selection of drinks, meals and snacks available from our Courtyard Bar and Cafeteria. Buffets and Childrens' Activity Birthday Parties all available on request.Creche facilities also available. INSOMNIAC SPORTS. MON - SAT 7.15am to 10am. All dry sports facilities available on request.

Figure 1.10 Leisure centres now offer a wide range of activities for all age groups

assorted outdoor activities under one roof, with light and heat provided.

The early leisure centres were established in the centre of towns so that they were easy for most people to get to. However, their position restricted any expansion so it was found that they were limited in the activities they could provide.

Despite some of the limiting effects there was significant interest in the indoor arenas and they continued to grow. Research reports such as the Wolfenden publication *Sport and the Community* did much to enhance the design and provision of the new breed of leisure centres and the 1970s saw virtually every local authority building leisure centres with surrounding tracks and field areas as well as other traditional activity areas such as tennis, football and netball.

Let us now expand our list under these headings in order to establish what is available in your area and also the range of provision such as accommodation, dining and entertainment:

- *Private sector leisure*

Health clubs	Hotels
Golf centres	Pubs
Football and rugby clubs	Restaurants
Cinemas	Bistros
Tennis and racquet clubs	Sports parks/zoos
Theme and amusement parks	

- *Public sector leisure*

Swimming pools	Public gardens
Museums	Play/swing areas
Country parks	Riverside areas
Playing fields	Stately homes
Community centres	Heritage trails
Educational centres	

- *Voluntary*
    Youth organizations
    Army Cadet Forces, Air Training Corps
    Amateur dramatic groups
    Cultural groups/arts and crafts
    Playgroups for children
    Disabled groups
    Youth clubs
    Religious groups

Figure 1.11

Leisure and lifestyle

From our lists under sector headings we can see that on occasions there will be some overlap of provision such as theatres, health clubs or squash courts that could each fall under public or private sectors. In many ways, this provision is being repeated because of demand and support within each of the markets and also budgets in the public sector being cut back, forcing them to adopt a more commercial approach.

People are continually looking to new forms of leisure pursuits. This is because of:

- New innovations, e.g. virtual reality games, quasar centres
- More leisure time
- Greater disposable income
- Cheaper travel.

Leisure in the home has also changed. The advent of television saw a shift from the cinema, and video furthered its demise (the end of widespread popularity). However, surveys since about 1989 show how the multiplex cinemas have won back audiences with a more compact range of services, to include restaurants and bars as well as a wider choice of films.

Leisure in the home has not just been limited to games and television. The advent of exercise and fitness equipment designed for home use has seen an increase in exercise activities in the privacy of the garage or bedroom. Fitness videos have created a 'home army' of participants striving for perfect bodies and lifestyles to match. Computer games such as the Sega range have created a virtual cult in home entertainment. Karaoke machinery, camcorders and improved quality of hi-fi and compact discs have given a home option to consumers for entertainment.

The national leisure and tourism scene

In order to give some background to developments, the following pages include details of consumer spending and preferences in leisure activities, holidays and tourism.

From Figure 1.12 we can see how people are spending their disposable income. It is clear that holidays overseas, neighbourhood leisure, eating out and home entertainment figure highly. Alcohol too forms a large part of expenditure but can be altered by taxation either up or down. Hobbies and pastimes is a category which requires monitoring, as expenditure here may overlap with some of the other activities such as home entertainment. In Table 1.2 the major leisure activity markets are put into rank order. It is worth noting that statistical research was only available up to 1989, so there may be some slight differences in research published later than this.

Established major markets

Despite considerable variations in market growth, the sectors that receive the bulk of leisure spending did not change during the 1980s. The business is still dominated by eating out, holidays overseas, DIY and the main elements in the alcohol market.

Task 1.6

Conduct a mini survey on how many hours a week your family and friends spend watching TV and videos. Produce your findings under age-group headings, e.g. 0–10 years, 10–17 years, 17–21 years, 21 + years.

You may also want to survey visits to cinemas as compared with watching videos.

Compare your findings with Table 1.3.
Element 1.1, PC6

Table 1.1 Some key leisure indicators

		1979	1984	1989	% change 1979–89
Home-based leisure					
Books published, no. of titles	000	41	50	61	+49
Households with second colour TV	%	7	18	47	+571
Households with video	%	1	35	65	+6500
Compact discs deliveries	Millions	nil	1	42	from nil
Number of home owners	Millions	10.6	12.5	14.6	+38
Households with video camera	Millions	0.01	0.2	0.8	+8000
Eating and drinking					
Adults eating out	Millions	18.0	21.2	24.9	+38
Wine consumption per adult	Litres	11.0	13.8	16.6	+51
Neighbourhood leisure					
Cinemas admissions	Millions	112	53	96	−14
Football League attendances	Millions	25	18	20	−20
Betting shops	000	12.5	10.9	10	−20
Adults taking part in active indoor sports	Millions	9.8	12.4	13.2	+35
Holidays and tourism					
Visits to attractions	Millions	224	238	287	+28
Short holiday trips in GB by British residents	Millions	29	38	38	+31
Adults taking holidays overseas	%	20	28	33	+65
Foreign visitors to UK	Millions	12.5	13.6	17.2	+38
Households with car	%	58	61	67	+16

Source: Martin and Mason, Leisure Consultants

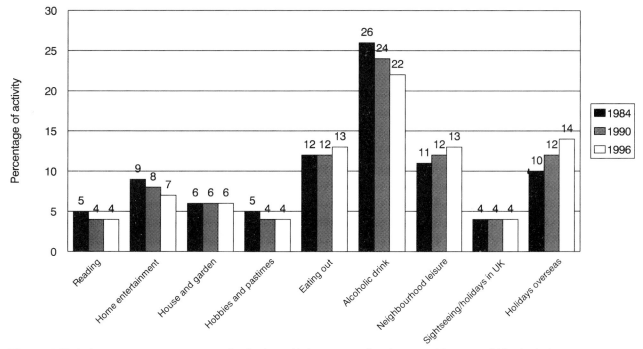

Figure 1.12 Leisure money: percentage distribution of leisure spending (*source*: Mason and Martin, Leisure Consultants)

Table 1.2 The major events

Value of spending	£bn	1989 Rank	£bn	1979 Rank
Eating out	11.3	1	13.9	2
Beer	10.7	2	4.7	1
Holidays overseas	10.4	3	2.6	3
Do-it-yourself	4.9	4	1.7	5
Spirits	4.6	5	2.5	4
Wine	4.5	6	1.6	6
Holiday accommodation in UK	3.9	7	1.5	8
Sport	3.3	8	1.2	10
Television	2.9	9	1.6	7
Gambling	2.9	10	1.3	9
Total of above	**59.4**		**22.6**	
All leisure spending	**77.8**		**29.0**	

Source: Martin & Mason, Leisure Consultants, 1990

Task 1.7

Eating out is proving to be on the increase as a leisure activity. Collect together details of how many restaurants there are in your immediate area (say a 10 mile radius). Having collected the details, classify them into Fast Food, Family, Pub, Wine Bar, Ethnic, etc. Conduct a survey of 50 people, of different age groups, asking which one or ones they frequent and produce a 'top 3' of all eating establishments in your area.
Element 1.2, PC3 and 5

Eating out, DIY, UK holiday accommodation and sport have moved up the rankings since 1979, but the top 10 market sectors are unchanged. Together they account for just over three-quarters of all leisure spending, only marginally less than a decade ago.

Two main growth areas

Further analysis indicates that, in terms of the volume of business, there have been two main growth areas in the leisure markets in the 1980s and 1990s:

- Home entertainment
- Overseas holidays.

Spending on both has more than doubled in real terms since 1979.

It is interesting to note that Table 1.2 changes the rank order of the activities. Eating out is seen to be number 1 activity per value if spent by the consumer. Note also the prime expansion areas of overseas holidays and home entertainment. The domestic markets have been quick to respond to the threat of overseas holidays by upgrading resort facilities. Thus we have seen the introduction of leisure and holiday worlds with leisure pools with tropical temperatures and the flexibility of opening, including weekend and midweek breaks off-season, promotions and many more enticements. But they still cannot guarantee the weather! To counteract the trend for home entertainment more and more pubs, clubs and restaurants are introducing offers such as:

- *Pubs with*
  - Cabaret and live artists
  - Quiz nights
  - Karaoke evenings
  - Guest beers
  - Satellite TV
- *Clubs with*
  - Reduced entry at early evening
  - Happy hour or doubles bars
  - Free entry party guests
  - Competitions – Lookalike, Wet T-shirt, New Faces
- *Restaurants with*
  - Reduced prices for early clients
  - Special children's meals
  - Extended menus to include offers
  - Introduction of privilege cards for regular diners

Task 1.8

What other forms of event or activity can you think of that would encourage customers? Suggest a further three or four that are not included in the book.
Element 1.2, PC1, 2 and 3

● *Pubs with restaurants and accommodation (as above but include)*
  – Accommodation offers
  – Weekend breaks
  – Function catering.

Despite all these attempts the home entertainment market continues to grow. In Table 1.3 we can see the breakdown of how the money is spent.

As leisure providers, it is important to study and react to such statistics, in order to ensure we keep our part of the business share of leisure or to create a new part. Within it Table 1.3 gives an overview of how leisure products and activities are taking place within the UK. Perhaps you can relate to the tables within the text to support your assignments or for your evidence building within college or school assignment activities.

Table 1.3

Market sub-sectors	RATIO of 1989 spending to 1979 spending at constant prices	VALUE of spending in 1989 (£ million)
Three completely new		
Compact audio discs	from nil	388
Home computer software etc.	from nil	272
Cable and satellite TV	from nil	178
The top ten growth market		
Pre-recorded video purchases	720	266
Home computer systems	110	280
Blank video cassettes	79	188
Pre-recorded video rentals	61	557
Electronic music keyboards	46	246
Video cameras	40	224
VCR rentals	35	769
VCR purchases	19	595
Video games software	9	67
Video games systems	6	45
Other markets where spending has at least doubled		
Pre-recorded audio cassettes	3.7	444
Colour TV set purchases	3.1	722
Electronic toys and games	2.5	100
In-car audio equipment	2.4	210
Table wine	2.4	3188
Audio equipment separates	2.2	235
Sparkling wine	2.1	314
Garden furniture etc.	2.1	218

Source: Martin and Mason, Leisure Consultants, 1990

Task 1.9

From Table 1.3, we can see that cable and satellite TV have increased their market spending from nil in 1979 to £178 million in 1989. Cable is being seen as a major provider not just for TV but also for other forms of communication, including phone lines to your home.

1 Establish who are the major providers of cable networks operating in the UK. (Visit a TV store to find out.)

2 Write to two of these to find out what is involved in installing cable to households.

3 What growth do the companies chosen see in cable and entertainment for the home? Are there any new aspects to cable other than TV?

Element 1.2, PC5

So far we have looked at the changing patterns of leisure and tourism activities under various categories. Our statistical tables give us a clear indication of how money and time is being spent in leisure pursuits. We now need to look at facilities, products and services which are offered by them.

Objectives of the products and services provided

In this section we will look at the objectives of facilities (their purpose and role) and how that affects how their products and services are targeted at ourselves the users. We shall also cover how different customers require different products and services, and how that affects confidentiality when holding information about clients and customers (Data Protection Act 1984). The need for health and safety of customers will also be covered.

As customers, very few of us are particularly concerned with the objectives of a local sports complex, cinema or travel agent, but we are concerned about how we are treated whilst with them. The value we get for the money we pay for their facilities and in certain circumstances the confidentiality they keep when we give out personal information to them are important to us. For example, when we seek membership at a private health club, it is possible that personal details about the following may be required:

● Health and physical condition
● Home address and telephone number
● Marital status
● Bank account details
● Next of kin (nearest relative).

The last thing we want is for this information to be circulated to health insurance companies, credit companies and mailshot businesses. If the information is circulated we may receive the junk mail we have all come to know and love. There are also more serious issues which we will look at later in the text.

In order for us as people working, or hoping to work, in the leisure and tourism industry to identify the objectives of a facility, we need to know what information they are giving out. By way of example, let us look at the following, both of which may be available in your local area:

● Leisure complex (public)
● Heritage centre

The leisure complex

Most of us have visited our local sport and recreation centre for a swim or game of badminton or squash. But very few of us have considered why such facilities are there, except that we enjoy using them. Imagine if they were not! What would you do? I dare say the answers would be varied to say the least.

Every local authority up and down the country is charged with providing the opportunity for *all citizens* to undertake recreational activities, in this example sport and recreation.

Task 1.10

How many leisure centres do you have in your local area? List the facilities you think they should have and compare with the actual, as published in their leaflets.
Element 1.1, PC4

The phrase 'all citizens' includes the less able and disabled. All local leisure centres are controlled by the local authority and often fall under the Department of Leisure and Tourism Services or similar. At present the government is cutting back its subsidy for local councils and encouraging them to take a more commercial approach and increase the number of customers through its leisure centre doors, whilst at the same time charging the 'going rate' for activities undertaken. Leisure centres are now involving themselves in:

● Function catering
● Commercial coaching and training for sport and qualifications linked to them
● Room hire for meetings
● Venues for exhibitions and display such as art, career opportunities and education
● Venues for craft fairs.

Some large centres are venues for events such as:

● Rock concerts
● Auctions
● Theatre productions and pantomime.

All of the above are not what we would normally expect when thinking of our local leisure centre, so it is important that the leisure centre makes us – the customer – aware of this by identifying its services and publishing them by way of:

● Press adverts
● Brochures
● Leaflets through the door.

Task 1.11

Conduct an investigation into how your local sports centre gets its message about facilities to present and potential customers. Are its objectives clear? If not, why not!
Element 1.1, PC4

The heritage centre

These days we have come to expect entertainment as part of our day out to a working museum or heritage centre. Competition is now present for our custom, whether it be free of charge or paying at the gate. Historical attractions are now packaged in a modern way and it is important that the customer knows what to expect if he or she, a group, or class of pupils is to visit them. Learning should be fun, and that is the message to put across. Various methods are being used such as:

● Glossy advertising brochures
● Free talks to parties
● Videos about the centre
● Live actors in real-life settings as in working museums or heritage centres
● Costume hire – visitors can try on period costume and pose for photographs
● Quizzes and trails about the centre for children.

And many more!

The objectives of the heritage centre have changed tremendously and there is a lot of money to be made from a historical past. But it is important that the centres are interesting, fun and provide other services such as

THE FESTIVAL

Divided Loyalties is a major festival commemorating Chester's role in the English Civil War. From July 1994 to September 1995 the excitement and drama of the 17th century will be vividly recreated in one of Britain's leading Civil War cities.

The Civil War

The English Civil War of 1642 to 1651 was one of the most turbulent chapters in British history. The bloody conflict between King Charles I and his Parliament divided the nation, touching the lives of every man, woman and child.

Civil War Chester

As a key Royalist stronghold, Chester played a significant role in these times of crisis. The city suffered a long and devastating siege between 1642 and 1646. King Charles himself visited Chester in September 1645 only to witness the defeat of his army at the nearby Battle of Rowton Moor.

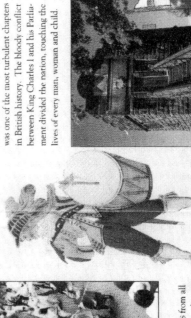

OVER 70 ORGANISATIONS from all sections of the community have come together to create an ambitious and colourful city-wide festival for all the family.

Chester's spectacular Civil War heritage becomes the setting for a varied programme of themed events including
- battle re-enactments • living history
- street theatre and pageantry
- music and drama • exhibitions
- traditional crafts • guided tours
- educational activities

Figure 1.13 A local heritage activity

refreshments, toys/souvenirs and fact packs. Above all, in your entrance fee you are paying for VFM (value for money).

Question

How do these examples compare with facilities in your own area?

Leisure and tourism facilities, whether national or local, tend to rely on each other in order to be successful in business.

Task 1.12

Make a list of as many businesses as you can think of which would be connected with the tourism industry in your own area.
Element 1.2, PC2, 3 and 5

Well, how did you get on? I suppose you included the following:

- Hotels
- Guest houses
- Public houses
- Restaurants
- Amusement parks.

I hope you also included:

- Coach operators
- Tourist information offices
- Theatres
- Art and craft shops
- Museums.

And if you live by the coast:

- Beach businesses such as windsurfing, boat hire and fishing trips
- Fairgrounds and theme parks.

There are also a number of specific areas which attract tourists. These are:

- Historical sites
- Places of natural beauty
- National Trust properties.

As you can see, there are quite a number of interested parties involved, all trying to attract the business of the tourist as well as local people. How can they help each other? Well, at first glance you would think they can't and, indeed, not all can. However, it is possible for a few of them. Let us look more closely.

Case study

The Nelson is a thirty-bedroomed hotel situated in the Cornish town of Looe, a pretty coastal port with lots of shops and good parking space for the visitor.

There is little problem in filling the hotel with guests during the summer, but trying to get trade during the rest of the year is a different matter. So the owner gave it some thought. Why do people come in the summer and what sort of visitor does the hotel get?

Answer

In the summer it is a natural attraction. Looe is a beauty spot by the coast with nice beaches and caves, good restaurants and lots of interests to keep the kids happy. The type of guests attracted are mature couples and young families, very few single visitors or single couples. Guests tend to visit from May through to September.

How can the Nelson increase its trade?

Answer

By catering for specific groups, such as:

- Fishing clubs
- Amateur art groups
- History societies.

The town of Looe has great fishing, but with trawlermen in port three days a week there are plenty of boats lying idle. So there is the prospect of hiring out their boats for fishing parties.

Amateur art groups would find the area excellent for painting the rugged coastline, interesting buildings, the boats and sea birds, etc., all of which are ideal for capture on canvas.

Cornwall is full of history, with its smuggling past, the wreckers who lived in the coastal towns, Camelot and King Arthur, Merlin and Guinevere – a myth but nonetheless still a tourist attraction.

As you can see, the prospect of mini-breaks revolving around specific interest groups was the answer, but assistance from other businesses was also required. Since they were in the same situation, it was not difficult to enlist support.

The coach company was only too glad to pick up visitors from the station and transport groups who were staying at the hotel, at a cheap rate of course!

The trawlermen would lease their boats for up to two days and would pilot and navigate the fishing clubs to the best fishing sites. They would also ferry the historical groups around the coastline to see smugglers' caves and wrecking sites.

The local art museum offered to give talks on the natural beauty spots around the area of Looe. This was particularly good for amateur artists who did not know the area too well. The museum also offered to conduct clay potting classes whilst guests were at the hotel (for a nominal fee). Whilst all this was happening, the Nelson was:

- Filling its rooms
- Filling its restaurant, at breakfast and dinner
- Providing packed lunches for the guests
- Providing entertainment whilst guests were buying drinks at the bar

- Keeping staff employed during the autumn and early spring
- Keeping the coach operators happy
- Keeping the trawlermen happy
- Increasing turnover for the local museum.

And, above all, keeping itself open.

Task 1.13

In groups of two, think of any other packages the Nelson Hotel could offer to increase its business during weekdays in the autumn, winter and early spring. From what other areas of competition would the Nelson's business be exposed? And what would the mutual benefits be to the hotel and other businesses?
Element 1.2, PC5

Unit assignments

Having completed the first section of the textbook, it would be useful now to undertake an assignment in order for you to generate evidence for your portfolio. This evidence will assist in covering performance criteria for the first element of the unit.

It will also give you the opportunity to cover some of the core skills required in communication, application of numbers and information technology.

Note: You will find assignments at the end of each section within the textbook. There is an accompanying tutor resource pack for all the assignments within the book, which provides further material to assist you in the coverage of the assignments. You may wish to discuss your action plan around the resource materials with your tutor, as some of the assignments are best conducted in pairs or groups. There are, however, plenty of opportunities for individual work.

▪ Assignment 1.1 ▪

This assignment is made up of three parts:

Part 1 – An explanation of the meaning of leisure and tourism and the various parts (contexts that form it).

Part 2 – An investigation into leisure and tourism products and facilities linked to a comparison within your local area and those provided nationally.

Part 3 – A study of various sectors of the leisure and tourism industry and the facilities provided by them.

Coverage of all three parts will be best conducted by undertaking a series of tasks which are listed in sequence in order to help you.

Coverage

- Element 1.1
- Performance Criteria 1 to 5
- Core Skills opportunities
  Communications
  Application of numbers
  Information technology

It is anticipated that most, if not all, of the range statements will also be covered.

Task 1

Using the Glossary in the GNVQ Unit Handbook, provide in your own words an explanation of the term 'leisure and tourism'. (In order to do this, you may wish to ask people working in the industry for their understanding of the term.)

Task 2

Again using the GNVQ Glossary, provide a list of as many leisure and tourism facilities you can think of under the different 'contexts' headings.

Task 3

Using the information provided under Task 2, look at your list and establish which of the facilities under each context are provided in your own local area and those which are not.

Task 4

Having established the facilities which are not available in your local area, try to find out where they are available and why they are available. (This may involve you in writing to local councils in other areas or contacting large companies involved in leisure and tourism nationally.) Try to get as much literature and information as you can in order to make a better comparison.

Task 5

Using the GNVQ Glossary for 'sectors' in the leisure and tourism industry, provide a list of three facilities or services under each sector (refer to your list under Task 2 for help). From your study so far indicate on your list those facilities or services which are provided locally and nationally.

Task 6

Conclude your assignment with an overall report on your comparisons of products, services and facilities provided in your local area with those provided nationally. What are the major differences?

All your work should be word processed.

Factors which affect demand for products and services

The common needs of different types of customer

In this section we need to look at what are the most common requirements of our visitors and customers when visiting a facility. Before we do that, however, let us establish the types of customers we can expect to deal with:

- *Existing customers* – those who you know and generally know what they require.

- *Potential customers* – here you do not know them but you will need to identify what they want and how or whether you can provide it.

Customers also come in different categories, such as:

- *Pleasure* – here the customers only wish to enjoy themselves and will have needs based around personal enjoyment.

- *Business* – all customers are our business, but some of them are conducting their business whilst with us. Here detail is required and what you promise, you must deliver. A negative effect on the customer's business can be caused because of your failure to deliver and will undoubtedly have the same effect on yours.

- *Groups* – here we need to cater for a variety of needs. They could be diet, physical disability, transportation, accommodation and communication, to name a few.

- *Individuals* – here needs may be mixed. They may include privacy or pleasure, but it is important to identify and cater for them. Individuals may need special attention, such as a young person travelling on their own.

Identifying customers' needs is the key to any successful operation, whether it be a public, private or commercial event.

Task 1.14

List the needs of a lone businessman staying at a city centre hotel, who will be attending a two-day conference at a venue nearby but not at the hotel itself.
Element 1.1, PC6

Customers' needs and expectations differ and are dependent on what capacity they are in and the activities they are undertaking, such as a:

● Client
● Customer
● Guest
● Tourist.

If you were a visitor to another city or town you would normally be able to find your way around by consulting a map, visiting an information centre or simply by asking someone in the street. But what if you were a foreign visitor, or you visit a foreign country? What would your needs be then? Possibly the following:

● The services of a tourist representative at your hotel
● Details of travel arrangements from your hotel, to include:
  – Coaches
  – Excursions
  – Private
  – Public
  plus departures and arrival times
● Details of attractions, scenic spots, historical sites, etc., in the surrounding area
● Facilities provided by the hotel, such as:
  – Entertainment
  – Leisure facilities
  – Meals and meal times
● Medical services in the event of an emergency

● Details of shops, markets or special auctions taking place during your stay
● Details of social customs: the do's and don'ts when dealing with local people.

There are probably many more, depending on individual interests or necessities, for example someone physically disabled or visually impaired, someone with specific dietary requirements or merely someone who wants to sit with a good book and relax by the hotel pool (assuming it has one).

In the introduction to the book we discussed how the world is becoming smaller with the advent of improved and faster transportation. We are now seeing a much wider range of visitors to our country, whether it be for business or pleasure. Successful operations are catering for a wider range of needs for our visiting public, giving attention to aspects such as:

● Good signposting
● Multi-language literature for tours, attractions and facilities offered to tourists
● Audio tapes in different languages at attractions, museums, etc.
● Increased range of meals offered in restaurants to cater for ethnic as well as religious requirements
● Details of transport to venues and quickest routes to take
● Customized bookings for groups of travellers
● Additional services for business tourists, such as secretarial support, drivers and chauffeurs with a car and tour itineraries for accompanying guests.

The UK is seeing for the first time a land link with Europe through the Channel Tunnel. Forecasters are suggesting a tremendous increase in European visitors to the UK in general, and not just to the traditional venues of London and the Roman historical centres such as Chester and York. Manchester is just 6½ hours from Paris by the Euro train link. How are leisure and tourism providers in the UK preparing for such a business prospect?

Figure 1.14

Task 1.15

Visit your local Department of Tourism and Leisure Services and find out what information is available for European visitors to the area. Find out also if your area is being promoted in Europe, and if so how?
Element 1.2, PC2 and 5

Matching customers' needs with products and services

The implications of demand will depend on whether the facility is providing services for:

- Local visitors/customers
- Non-paying customers
- Paying customers
- Tourists and non-local visitors.

The type of visitors will also have a bearing on how the facility caters for the needs of customers, for example:

- Disabled
- Families
- Senior citizens
- Visually impaired
- Young persons
- Large groups, such as conference delegates
- Educational groups, such as a party of students.

Customer demand – is it being satisfied?

What must be clear to prospective customers is exactly what is offered by the facility. We discussed this point when we looked at the types of facilities in the previous section. However, we now need to look at the advertised objectives of facilities, as the customers' expectations are the facilities' demand. Look at the Granada Studios Tour literature.

GREAT ATTRACTIONS THAT MAKE YOUR DAY

1. **BACKSTAGE TOUR** – see what's behind your favourite programmes. **(30 MINS)**
2. **SOUNDSTAGE TOUR** – see the famous sets come to life. **(30 MINS)**
3. **THE BAKER STREET VICTORIAN EXTRAVAGANZA.**
4. **THE CORONATION ST. EXPERIENCE** – programme history and the hallowed cobbles. **(CONTINUOUS)**
5. **SOUND EFFECTS SHOW. (30 MINS)**
6. **THE HILARIOUS HOUSE OF COMMONS DEBATE. (30 MINS)**
7. **THE SOOTY SHOW. (30 MINS)**
8. **DOWNTOWN NEW YORK.**
9. **UFO ZONE** – a nail biting voyage into an alien spacecraft. **(CONTINUOUS RIDES)**

BRAND NEW FOR '95

10. **ROBOCOP: THE RIDE** – a thrilling new experience on MotionMaster, our futuristic computer simulator ride. **(CONTINUOUS RIDES)**
11. **HAUNTS OF THE OLDE COUNTRY** – European premiere of a truly spooky 3-D show. **(APPROX 20 MINS)**
12. **3-D ROCK LASER SHOW** – a spectacular 3-dimensional high powered laser display accompanied by great rock tunes. **(15 MINS)**
13. **DEADLY EFFECTS** – gory special effects straight from the horror movies. **(30 MINS)**
14. **CORONATION STREET STUDIO SETS** – famous interior sets and a Street Star appearance on site every day.

Special Facilities.

We hope the following information will assist your movement around the site and enable you to visit every attraction. Should you need any further assistance please do not hesitate to contact any member of staff.

TOILETS
Disabled facilities are situated in the following areas:
New York Street
Exhibition Hall, upper level
Stables Restaurant, Grape Street
Deerstalker Pub, Baker Street

LIFTS
A lift is situated inside the New York De Vere Hotel, for access to upper level.

SHOWS
There is disabled access to all shows on site, as follows:–

UFO Zone:	Via entrance ramp on Grape Street.
MotionMaster:	Although this attraction cannot be ridden by disabled guests, the film may be viewed from a stationary position.
The Sooty Show:	In New York Projections, disabled access via ramp.
House of Commons/ 3D Show:	Via lift in entrance of De Vere Hotel, up to Exhibition Hall.
Sound Effects Show/ Make-Up Show:	Situated on ground level.

Access Coronation Street via lift in New York De Vere Hotel and through Baker Street set.

EXIT
When you are ready to leave the grounds please make your way to the main entrance gate, which will be opened for you.

BABY CHANGING
New York Street
Stables Restaurant, Grape Street
Rovers Return Pub

TELEPHONES
New York Street
Coronation Street
Rovers Return Pub

PHOTOGRAPHY
Photography of the Tour is encouraged. Free camera hire courtesy of Kodak is available from Laughing Stock on New York Street. Films are sold in all our shops.

Figure 1.15 (a) Granada Studios Tour literature

(b)

(c)

Figure 1.15 (b) Granada Studios Tour logo;
(c) Coronation Street

Customers' needs and expectations must be met if any facility is to be run successfully, and customers' demands met. The objectives stated by an attraction, museum, or hotel must be clear and evident to prospective customers.

Task 1.17

1 Seaworld is a new attraction in your area. Describe what you think should be the objectives of Seaworld, in order to cater for a varied range of visitors.
2 List what you and your group or friends' expectations would be from an establishment called Seaworld. What facilities would you expect to cater for a varied range of customers' needs?
3 Design a leaflet promoting Seaworld. Include in the literature what facilities and services you think should be included to cater for a varied range of visitors.
Element 1.2, PC1, 2 and 3

Task 1.16

- *What facilities are offered to visitors at Granada Studios Tour?*
- *What additional facilities may be offered to special groups?*
- *What is the typical age range of visitors?*
- *What amount of time would you need to allow for a visit taking in all the attractions?*
- *Are there any additional costs apart from admission charges?*
Element 1.2, PC1, 2 and 3

Task 1.18

Choose advertising literature from two different facilities in your local area.

Before reading through them, list what your demands would be of establishments such as the one chosen. Compare your list with the stated facilities in the literature. How do they compare?

Finally, visit the chosen facilities and judge for yourself. Do the differences (if any) make for more or less enjoyment?
Element 1.2, PC1, 2 and 3

Health and safety issues

In this section we will look at how health and safety issues can be affected by meeting people's needs and expectations.

Most of us at some time will be involved in travelling on a boat, train or aeroplane. Some of us may have hidden fears about doing so. Most of us have known some people who are afraid of flying or sailing.

Trains generally do not present a problem, though recently there were a few people killed by falling from a train when it was travelling at high speed. It happened in one particular spot around Tamworth, known at the time as the 'Tamworth Triangle'. The problem was that passengers were thought to be standing by the train doors or putting their heads out of the window, whilst holding on to the door-opening handle and in turn causing the door to open – a tragic accident. British Rail have now fitted central locking on their Inter City high speed trains. This is just one example of how operators respond to a situation in order to ensure the health and safety of their customers.

Generally airline companies and airports work closely together to ensure the safety of their passengers. This involves a great deal of monitoring and security, and can at times result in frustration for passengers, who have to check in early, sometimes up to two hours before their flights. They then have to queue in line to be searched and their luggage scanned and suffer the occasional embarrassment when their luggage is searched because the scanner has picked up their gas hair-curler or camera with the batteries still in. Nobody likes their underwear displayed to the world.

But really this is a small price to pay when you think of the consequences of not doing

thorough checks – such as the Lockerbie air disaster and the terrorist attack at Frankfurt airport in 1982. Health and safety issues are paramount for operators within the leisure and tourism industry – health and safety does not come cheap.

Task 1.19

Arrange a visit to your local Football League club, and enquire as to what are the financial implications of the Taylor Report on health and safety at football grounds. What measures have been taken and what measures are still to be taken by the club?

Element 1.1, range products and services

Note: The Taylor Report followed the Hillsborough disaster in 1989, when over 90 Liverpool Football Club fans were killed in a tragic accident caused by overcrowding in an area of the stadium at Sheffield Wednesday football ground. The Bradford football ground fire of 1985 was also a contributory factor that brought about wholesale changes that were to lead to the Taylor Report.

Read the articles from *Leisure Opportunities*, 21 October 1994.

At present there are issues on the compulsory fitting of seatbelts in minibuses and coaches due to the incidence of accidents involving buses and coaches without them. Public opinion is moving towards having it made compulsory, but is the public equally keen to absorb costs?

STAND COLLAPSES AT CONCERT

Around 30 people were taken to hospital last week after a temporary stand collapsed at the Earls Court Exhibition Centre during a Pink Floyd concert.

The 20ft high stand, which had been erected by Arena Seating, had been cleared for use by the local authority's safety inspectors the previous morning.

The stand, which was supported by scaffolding, was holding 1,200 fans who triggered the collapse when they stood up to welcome the band on stage.

Victims said the whole stand tilted forward throwing some people 20–30ft to the ground, and then caved in like a concertina.

"We have used Arena Seating at Earls Court and Olympia many, many times in the past," said halls managing director Doug Littlejohns. "We are completely mystified as to why this accident happened."

The Health and Safety Executive is carrying out an inspection of the stand.

The incident took place on the same night as Channel 4 screened a *Dispatches* documentary on safety in stands at public events, particularly football matches. The exposé showed flaws at Premiership and Football League clubs despite the recommendations on safety made after the Bradford fire in 1985 and the Hillsborough disaster in 1989.

Standing up for safety

Stadium and arena operators are awaiting the results of the inquiry into the collapse of a section of a temporary stand at Earls Court on 12 October. Thirty-six people were taken to hospital with shock, bruising, and in the most severe cases, back injuries. All have now been released.

The collapse occurred at the beginning of a Pink Floyd concert as the crowd stood to welcome the band. The 20ft high stand, which was holding around 1,200 people, had been cleared for use by the Royal Borough of Kensington and Chelsea's safety inspectors the night before. The concert was cancelled and held on 17 October.

Accidents like this, which occur in spite of stands having passed current inspections, are an operator's worst nightmare. They have a detrimental effect on all events and also a dangerous habit of becoming confused in the public's mind with every other incident which has occurred in a public space, giving an impression that the industry is inherently unsafe. This is obviously the last thing the stadia and arenas market needs, as it battles to keep the volume of business up in the face of rising costs and pressurised profit margins. While the market awaits the outcome of the investigation into the cause of the accident, the issue of safety in leisure settings is being reviewed by a number of operators and councils.

There is still some confusion in the market about the standards required by the licensing body for both indoor and outdoor events, and also about the guidelines which exist to ensure satisfactory safety standards are adhered to. The publication of the *Guide to Health, Safety and Welfare at Pop Concerts and Similar Events*, more commonly known as the 'Pop Code', in 1993 was intended to standardise the safety requirements under which events are operated and to lead to a consistency of enforcement approach across the country.

There are still operators who believe that the pop code only applies to outdoor events when it does, in fact, cover both indoor and outdoor events in the finest detail. The code was published by the Health and Safety Commission, the Home Office and the Scottish Office following extensive consultation and thorough reviews of a wide range of events from large outdoor concerts to smaller indoor gatherings. This information was used to develop the document which is exhaustive in its coverage of the safety issues involved with staging any public event.

The aim of the pop code was to create a document which could be used by both the operators of events and the inspectors, creating a collaborative approach to improving standards and ensuring that requirements were clearly set out in black and white.

One thing which is sometimes overlooked in these circumstances is the fact that individual managers are personally liable for errors which occur as a result of their negligence and which subsequently result in an accident. Such actions are brought through the criminal courts, meaning that custodial sentences are a possibility for the most serious misdemenour. Individuals are not protected from the law by their status as employees, meaning that they have every incentive to ensure that safety measures are adhered to scrupulously.

Liz Terry, Editor

Figure 1.16 Two articles from *Leisure Opportunities*, 21 October 1994 (copyright of Dicestar 93, tel: 01462 431385)

Task 1.20

Earlier in the section we discussed some passengers' fears about travelling. We said that, in general, trains were not a problem. But what about the 22½ miles of railway tunnel running under the English Channel? What health and safety measures are Eurotunnel implementing for their passengers? Write and ask for the literature they are issuing to passengers. On receiving it would you feel easier about using it as against the ferry or plane? Ask your other group members about their feelings.
Element 1.2, PC2 and 3

Security

This is part of health and safety. We have discussed what airlines and airports do to ensure that there are no risks to their passengers and their luggage and personal possessions, but what of other areas?

Task 1.21

Find out what measures are undertaken to ensure the security of customers' property in the following facilities:

- *City centre hotel*
- *Coach terminal*
- *Community sport and recreation centre*
- *Railway station*

Are details regarding the property of customers indicated by notices or written instructions to the customer?
Element 1.2, PC2 and 3

The health, safety and security of customers is all part of good customer care. As you read the customer care section of the book, you will no doubt be able to relate to areas we have discussed.

Confidentiality of information and security of facilities

Earlier in this section, under products and services provided by a facility, we looked at an example where confidentiality of personal information was an important factor in keeping the trust and loyalty of the customer. A vital part of the role of people in the leisure and tourism industry, in fact, is discretion and ensuring good customer relations.

Question

How many situations can you think of in a leisure and tourism aspect where a customer's confidentiality is particularly important?

Let us list some:

- Health and fitness clubs – membership details
- Health farms and clinics
- Hotel (as a guest)
- Passenger listing on a boat or aeroplane
- Restaurant or diner's club.

Why, you may ask. Well, many prominent people visit such establishments or travel in such a capacity. Everybody is entitled to privacy of some kind. Where confidentiality is breached it can put a person, such as a politician, film star, TV personality or a member of the Royal Family, in a position of embarrassment or, worse, a position of danger.

How many times in the popular press have we seen invasion of privacy via photographs of personalities and members of the Royal Family going about their private lives published in the newspaper with no opportunity to have them stopped? How would you feel about such an incident involving yourself, particularly if all you wanted to do was to relax or take some exercise or travel and enjoy a holiday without fear of invasion of your space or privacy?

The point may seem laboured but without respecting people's confidentiality, the idle remark or slip of the tongue could cost the establishment that individual's membership, and that of others when they found out about it, which in turn would have a disastrous effect upon the reputation of the health farm, clinic, restaurant or hotel.

Linked with confidentiality is the concept of security. Security can involve:

- Personal details about clients, such as:
  - Address
  - Telephone numbers
- Storage of valuable goods or personal items. This may be for a short period whilst within the establishment or for a longer period, for example when someone donates or loans a valuable piece of pottery, china or a painting to a museum or society
- Personal security. Important visitors may require additional security on the establishment, working with other agencies to include national security officers where there may be a risk of personal danger to that person. Examples of this would include:
  - Persons of exceptional wealth
  - Prominent politicians
  - Royal Family.

Task 1.22

Taking the health farm as an example, list some of the points you would include in talking to staff about the confidentiality and security of guests who are staying with your establishment. Assume a varied range of clients, e.g. personalities, politicians and everyday members of the public.
Element 1.2, PC2 and 3

Task 1.23

From the following areas of the leisure and tourism industry:

- *Travel operators*
- *Sport and recreation*
- *Hotels and catering*
- *Arts and entertainment*

choose two and carry out some limited research. Choose one person from each area and seek permission to obtain the following information:

Why did they choose their career in that area of leisure and tourism?
What are the advantages of their job?
What are the disadvantages of their job?
What qualifications were necessary to obtain their job?
What personal qualities do they feel are important in that job?
What advice would they give to someone starting out in their career in their area of work?

Note: *This information may be discovered at an interview with the individual or by writing to them.*

Don't forget to thank all concerned!
Element 1.3, PC2

In the section we look at the impact and economic significance that leisure and tourism activities have on an area. To assist in giving range to the concept, we will look at it under the following headings:

- Positive aspects
- Negative aspects
- Economic significance
- Social aspects
- Environmental impact on an area.

Positive aspects

Leisure and tourism activities can assist an area in raising its profile within the local, national and international arena. This helps to create more business for the immediate community and in turn creates employment for the local population. A lot depends on the interest value of the area. This can be determined by:

- Climate e.g. Torquay on the south coast
- Attractions – natural and man made e.g. Blackpool Pleasure Beach
- Heritage – the history and historical significance of the area
- Geography – its location near large towns e.g. Chester Zoo
- Transport connections – road, rail and air links e.g. Manchester Airport
- Accommodation – hotels, motels, caravan parks and camping facilities e.g. Disney Hotels.

Not all the factors are a priority but a mix will usually determine whether a person will visit an area. Other positive aspects are that where a tourist destination is popular, it tends to attract further investment to enhance amenities which can be used by the local population 'out of season' such as:

- Leisure centres
- Cinemas
- Shops
- Parks
- Restaurants.

All the activities of a successful tourist destination create a 'local wealth' and prosperity for the people who live there. This wealth in turn creates a need for better housing and local amenities, such as health care, leisure facilities, gardens and recreation areas. This helps to raise the status of an area and in turn its influence in the 'marketing' of the area to possible new markets in the local and national arena.

Negative aspects

Unfortunately there are always penalties or mildly put 'inconveniences' to put up with in an area where a large number of tourists visit. These can be summarized as follows:

- Increased traffic causing congestion
- Decreased parking space for local people
- Problems of noise – people enjoying themselves tend not to do it 'quietly'
- Increased litter and graffiti
- Erosion of natural beauty spots
- Pollution by way of increased traffic and exhaust fumes
- Increased local taxation of local residents, who have to pay higher water rates and, in the UK, increased business rates.

A combination of all these factors can create additional 'stress' on the local population and possible resentment towards tourists. This in turn can send a negative message to visitors. There is a fine balance between the benefits and the drawbacks for the local population in a popular tourist area. This balance is called the 'Multiplier Effect', which is to say that as long as people are employed, earning good salaries, spending in the local community along with the tourists, everybody enjoys a state of balance, otherwise chaos! Remember the old saying 'We don't need tourists we need tourism'.

The following is an extract from an opinion poll carried out in a Swiss resort. The findings speak for themselves.

People only think of money now	79%
The sense of community has been lost	53%
There are too many strangers	46%
The appearance of the village has been spoilt	45%
Family life has suffered	44%
The landscape has been ruined	43%
Only a few have benefited from tourism	26%

Source – The Holidaymakers, Jost Krippendorf (1994)

Economic aspects

We have mentioned the benefits to the local economy in the previous headings, however, there is a much wider benefit to a national economy where tourism plays a major part in the country's balance of payments. Countries such as Spain, Greece and Portugal rely heavily on the income generated from tourism because their manufacturing industries cannot employ the whole population. Geographically the climate of these countries is more suitable to an agricultural base, such as growing grapes for making wine or olive growing to make oil. These countries have large coastal regions which because of their climate are more suitable to the concept of 'sun, sand and sea' economies. Labour costs are low which in turn attracts tourist businesses to the region.

It is not just the resort that benefits from the tourist, other partners in the tourist industry also rely equally on the tourism of the region, for example:

● Transport such as taxis and coach operators
● Car hire firms
● Suppliers to the hotels and restaurants
● Souvenir shops
● Art and craft shops
● Tourist attractions not in the immediate area.

All in all the income generated from tourism in countries such as those mentioned plays a significant part in the wealth and prosperity of that country, but not necessarily the individual, as all too often the low labour costs do not help the local people to prosper. But their incomes do help to subsidise their 'non-seasonal' activities in other forms of employment.

Social aspects

This factor has been a source of study for a number of reasons, in particular, how tourism can affect the local community in its day-to-day life. Issues such as a sense of 'loss of identity' because the local people are always catering for other tourists' tastes and not their own.

In many towns in Spain the visitor will see 'real English pubs' or 'English food served here' accompanied by a photograph with fish, chips and peas on a plate. A sense of dissatisfaction can also be experienced as the local community is constantly exposed to other people's wealth which in turn can cause a sense of depression.

Home life too is disrupted where a family is reliant on work from hotels, restaurants etc. They have to work unsociable hours, where it is virtually impossible for the whole family to enjoy time together. A feeling of no control also may be experienced as events are dictated by others. The pace of life for the local community is also determined by the tourists and their tastes.

The social cost of tourism in a community has to be measured against the benefits and sometimes the price is too high. There is a new school of thought in major tourist areas of the world, where a more equal balance of cost to the community and cost to the tourist is being considered, we shall look with interest.

Task 1.24

Visit your local travel agent and ask them to explain the term 'Green Tourism'. Compare your responses from two travel centres – write down their answers for future assignments.
Element 1.2, PC4

Environmental aspects

This probably is the most sensitive issue in tourism today, the effects on the environment from tourism have to be weighed against short term gains or long term loss. How we deal with this problem will determine the inheritance we leave for our children.

There are inevitable costs to the environment from tourism activities such as:

- Changes to the landscape – the 'concrete jungle' experienced at major resorts by excessive building of multi-storey hotels and car parks
- Pollution in water – increased demands for water put on to sewage systems during the 'high season'
- Air quality – reduced because of increased traffic
- Increased noise – due to music, late night discotheques, traffic and large numbers of visitors
- Plant life – effects on plants and wild life, with erosion of 'habitat' can create the extinction of some species of plants and animals, or at the very least the urbanization of wild life such as foxes who become dependent on scavenging in refuse bins behind hotels and restaurants for food.

If environmental issues are not confronted at the planning stage of new tourist areas the result can be that the very attraction of the area can be destroyed.

Task 1.25

Visit your local Country Park and investigate how they 'manage people' e.g. encouraging visitors to take designated routes for walking and riding and how they try to educate people to look after their park!
Element 1.2, PC4

In order that we can investigate some of the aspects discussed so far, let us look into a recent issue affecting the tourist economy of the South Shore area of Blackpool.

Most of us know Blackpool – it is Britain's biggest resort with its 'Golden Mile' pleasure beach and famous tower. Its promenade stretches for miles and one of the many tourist pursuits is to take a tram ride to Bispham. The resort offers a tremendous range of activities and entertainment for families and the local hotels and guest houses depend on the tourist families for their livelihood.

Blackpool is always looking to extend its 'season' for holidaymakers and day visitors. One of the most successful attractions is the 'illuminations' which commence in September and finish in November, giving a boost to trade at a time when other resorts are trailing off in business. The illuminations extend for 4.5 miles along the length of the promenade in the South Shore.

Unfortunately, the upkeep and maintenance of the illuminations is extremely expensive and the local council have decided to reduce the area the illuminations extend to, in effect they stop at the start of the South Shore. This has created a great deal of protest from the hoteliers, guest house owners and restaurant proprietors, as they will lose business because of it. Visitors will not want to stay in or visit an area which does not have the attraction of the illuminations.

As you can see decisions made by local councils or at government level, can have major effects on the local economy of a tourist area, keeping a balance is always difficult.

Task 1.26

Every council has to produce a development plan for businesses in its area, this includes tourism, in short, a 'tourism strategy' – find out from your local Department of Leisure and Tourism what your area's tourism strategy is. Also, will it have any implications for loss or change of business for those established already like our Blackpool hoteliers.
Element 1.2, PC5

▪ Assignment 1.2 ▪

This assignment is made up of three parts:

Part 1

– A description of leisure and tourism products and services using the context headings of leisure, recreation, tourism and travel
– An explanation of what creates a demand for the products and services established under your context headings.

Part 2

– An investigation into the products and services provided in your local area
– An explanation as to whether the customers' demands are being met in your local area for the products and services provided.

Part 3

– A comparison of the products and services provided locally with those provided at the national level.

Notes

1 You are required to investigate two facilities from each of the contexts in order to provide breadth to your assignment.
2 Coverage of all three parts will be best conducted by undertaking a series of tasks which are listed in sequence, in order to help you. For reasons of space, five tasks are given here. These tasks are further detailed within the *Tutors Resource Pack* material.

Coverage

● Element 1.2
● Performance Criteria 1 to 5
● Core Skills opportunities
   Communications
   Application of numbers
   Information technology.

It is anticipated that most if not all of the Range statements will be covered.

Task 1

Provide a description of the leisure and tourism products and services found under the context headings of leisure, recreation, tourism and travel.

Task 2

Provide an explanation as to what creates a demand for the products and services you have listed under the context headings.

Task 3

Conduct an investigation as to the products and services which are provided in your local area. Remember to use the context headings as a guide. Provide your findings in a report style.

Task 4

Conclude your report with an indication as to what demands for products and services are being successfully met, and those which are not.

Task 5

Having established your report on local products and services, now undertake a comparison with one local and one national product and service. For each of the contexts include in your report the major differences and any differences created by different demands.

Employment opportunities

In this section we shall look at employment opportunities in leisure and tourism. We shall discuss the principal job roles of personnel involved, look at qualifications and skills required within leisure and tourism and what job roles are feasible for young people entering the industry.

Very few industries can match leisure and tourism for the variety of jobs it offers the young and not-so-young entrant: the possibility of providing a service in travel, accommodation, entertainment and leisure facilities for visitors, tourists and the general public, whether they be on day trips, weekend breaks or short residential stays.

You may choose a career from the following:

- *Outdoors* Maintaining gardens, historical sites, countryside parks and forest areas or caring for animals in a safari park or zoo.
- *In an office* Planning the travel arrangements for a package holiday for a tour operator or running the reception area for a caravan park or holiday village.
- *Overseas* As a resort representative on an exchange from a hotel training as anything from chef to receptionist to lounge waiter.
- *In a theatre* In charge of the lighting or scenery or marketing and publicity for the theatre.

- *In a seaport* Coordinating the activities of a roll-on-roll-off ferry terminal or working in the terminal as a hire car receptionist.
- *In an exhibition centre* Providing help and assistance for conference delegates or visitors to an exhibition.
- *Town centre* Working in the Tourist Information Office, helping visitors make their arrangements for accommodation, travel, entertainment.
- *In a museum* Helping build exhibit stands or covering for exhibits and paintings, assisting visitors, both local and foreign, with information.
- *In the air* Working as a cabin-crew member, assisting passengers as a steward or stewardess.
- *On the ground* As an airport receptionist working on behalf of an airline, taking bookings, issuing tickets and checking in passengers before their flights.
- *In a sports centre* In the office, planning events, managing activities and staff or in the sports hall, weights room, and swimming pool, supervising activities and maintaining the safety of customers and clients.

It is practically impossible to list all the hundreds of jobs we find in leisure and tourism, but over the next few pages we will look at some of them. However, for reasons of space only brief details will be given.

Hotels, catering and licensed trade

Depending on your chosen area of this part of the industry and the qualifications and experience you possess, it is possible to work as:

- Chef
- Conference and banqueting manager
- Hotel manager
- Hotel porter
- Receptionist
- Restaurant manager
- Room attendant
- Waiter or waitress.

Popular catering

- Call order chef
- Crew member (McDonald's, Wimpy, Burger King).

Licensed trade

Not everyone will play a part here as no person under 18 years of age will normally work in an area dispensing alcohol, but jobs include:

- Cellar management
- Cocktail bar person
- Lounge waiter
- Wine waiter or sommelier

The jobs mentioned can lead to you being a publican or licensee of your own public house, wine bar or brasserie.

Travel

Air

Most people immediately think of the air steward or stewardess. The vast majority of people see these staff as airbound waiters, which is not the case. Air stewards need to be able to handle any kind of emergency and initiate the appropriate safety procedures straight away. First aid skills, social skills and initiative are all qualities required by cabin staff.

Other aspects of air travel will include jobs such as:

- Airline manager
- Airline sales representative
- Airport manager.

Sea

Apart from the captain, navigators and engineers who are paramount to the running of the ship or ferry, staff in the following areas are needed:

- Bar persons
- Cabin waiter or steward
- Chef
- Entertainments manager
- Housekeeper
- Lounge waiter
- Purser

On shore

Ferry and hovercraft managers are required to observe the entrance and exit of vehicles onto their vessels in port and also to ensure that activities in the terminals run smoothly.

Road

Coach operators generally provide three types of supervisory role within the company:

- Private hire manager
- Tour manager
- Traffic manager.

National carriers, such as National Express, will also have:

- Stewards to serve food and refreshments to passengers
- Coach drivers – a skilled job requiring a PSV (Public Service Vehicle) licence to drive.

Rail

Jobs here would include:

- Buffet car waiter
- Dining car chef
- Guard
- Pullman class stewards and stewardesses
- Ticket inspector/conductor.

Some of the above roles would be interchangeable. In general the conductor and steward are seen as senior staff.

Travel agency staff

Travel staff work in agencies. This means that a company acts as a link between the general public and a service. Travel agencies then link prospective travellers with tour operators, transport services such as airlines, coaches and trains, and other businesses offering travel services, such as hotels. Travel agency staff include:

- Tour operator
- Business travel operator
- Incoming tour operator
- Reservations staff
- Couriers
- Resort representative
- Tourist guide.

Leisure facilities and entertainment

This area provides the most diverse range of job roles available and requires staff with a different range of experience and qualifications.

Cinema staff

- Bar staff
- Cashiers

- Cinema manager
- Projectionists
- Sales staff (confectionery, drinks, etc.)
- Usherettes.

The multiplex cinemas have created a heavy demand for such personnel.

Theatre staff

- Cashiers – box office manager
- Lighting technicians
- Manager
- Sales and marketing officer
- Scenery assistants.

Museums and art galleries

The advent of 'working museums' and museums of science and technology with working exhibits has brought about an expansion in this area. Museums geared to children, such as 'Eureka' at Halifax in Yorkshire and 'Catalyst' in Widnes, Cheshire, have resulted in families, groups and individuals visiting in greater numbers.

Figure 1.17 Interactive exhibit at the Catalyst Museum, Widnes, Cheshire

Staff who work in these areas include:

- Managers (sometimes referred to as curators, keepers or directors)
- Attendants
- Catering staff
- Sales and marketing staff
- Sales staff
- Security staff.

Historical property management

This is not the easy life that the tranquil surroundings of a heritage property and the lovely gardens might lead you to imagine. The manager is responsible for coordinating:

- Catering facilities
- Customer care
- Function facilities
- Health and safety
- Increasing visitor numbers
- Maintenance of the property, including the gardens
- Publicity
- Security.

Staff include:

- Caretakers
- Cleaners
- Ground staff
- Marketing and publicity staff
- Office staff
- Security staff.

Figure 1.18 National Trust logo

Zoos and wildlife parks

Animals need care and attention 365 days of the year, a challenging job for anyone. These operations require:

- Carers
- Marketing and publicity staff
- Sales staff.

Theme parks and tourist attractions

Major investment has been made in this area of leisure with companies recruiting staff in areas such as:

- Catering
- Customer liaison
- Entertainment
- Grounds maintenance
- Health and safety
- Maintenance
- Planning
- Publicity and marketing
- Security.

Sport and recreation

Again a very wide range of job roles in areas such as:

- Athletic stadiums
- Beauty therapy clinics
- Coaching centres
- Health and fitness clubs
- Health farms
- Local authority sports clubs
- Private sector
- Saunas and solariums
- Sports barns
- Swimming pools
- Tennis centres
- Weight training centres

to name a few!

Entry into this area of work, as with other areas, requires very specific qualifications before you may even be considered. We will discuss these in the next section.

Table 1.4

Job title	Background	Attributes
Sports centre attendant	• First point of entry into sport and recreation centres • Usually local authority • Activities would include assisting swimmers, cleaning pool and surrounds, supervising changing areas, moving and laying out equipment	• Minimum age 18 years, need to be a strong swimmer, possessing or nearly acquired Pool Life Guard Bronze Award • Must be prepared to work unsocial hours
Sales assistant – public sector leisure and tourism	• Persons wishing to start out in leisure and tourism sales would be working in the local office of the council, assisting with mailing, dealing with customers, staffing the TIO (Tourist Information Office)	• 17+ years, in receipt of GNVQ Intermediate qualification, ability to word process, good social skills
Travel agency clerk	• A courier in travel often starts here, organizing its stationery for clients, organizing the display shelves, undertaking duties required by the manager and occasionally assisting in the foreign currency unit	• 17+ years, GNVQ Intermediate, including some specific option or additional units, such as Researching Tourist Destinations and Travel Geography, good social skills and ability to work on their own
Gallery attendant	• Most museums and art galleries run by local councils require attendants to move and arrange displays, assist with routine maintenance and occasionally catalogue exhibits	• 17+ years, an interest in the arts, fit and able to work without supervision
Adventure holiday assistant	• These jobs may be seasonal and will be if undertaken in Europe or North America • Most companies will require employees to supervise young children or teenagers in sport and other leisure activites, whilst in their care	• 18+ years, GNVQ Intermediate, with some GCSE grades. A language qualification is also an advantage – especially if working in France, some companies require a driving licence, good leadership qualities, fitness and ability to work without supervision
Countryside ranger's assistant	• This job may involve you working locally or away from home • Country parks require constant maintenance and tending if natural resources such as ponds, lakes and coastal pathways • Essentially it is an outdoor job but may involve an employee undertaking clerical or office duties as required	• 18+ years, driving licence, GNVQ or City and Guilds qualification, preferably a conservation skill, such as stone wall building, fencing and/or paving included within the course, fit and with an interest in environmental and conservation issues
Events management (trainee)	• An increasing number of companies are now involving themselves in organizing sports and leisure events to include exhibitions – occasionally a vacancy exists for a trainee. Here the employee would be involved in a lot of fetching and carrying duties, but with the opportunity of observing more senior staff in operation, e.g. sales, planning and design • Staff enthusiasm and motivation plus undertaking other qualifications whilst in employment creates good opportunities in an expanding business	• 18+ years, driving licence essential. GCSE grades plus GNVQ Intermediate level qualification or equivalent. Good social skills, initiative and prepared to work unsociable hours. A liking for travel abroad would be required as some jobs will be out of your local area

New entrants

Over the previous pages you will have seen the vast range of jobs and responsibilities that need to be undertaken by people entering the leisure and tourism industry. A new entrant cannot expect to undertake a supervisory or management role straight away. It requires post-college training at every level, whether you leave with an Intermediate or Advanced GNVQ, Higher National Diploma, or Degree.

In order to help you to plan and identify roles within your present level of training, look at Table 1.4. The table is prepared as an indication and need not be viewed as a barrier to any job you wish to undertake. Motivation, personality and initiative very often count for more than qualifications, but qualifications do decide whether there will be the opportunity of an interview.

Job skills and qualities

As the leisure and tourism industry is made up of so many different areas of work it is very difficult to provide a common progression or career pathway for any one or group of individuals. What can be said is that there is commonality in the basic attributes (skills and qualities) of people working within the industry.

Our industry is about people – without them we are simply out of work. Taking this theme, if we wish to progress within the leisure and tourism industry the following skills and qualities will be required (as well as specific skills and qualifications dependent on the job):

- **Enthusiasm** A fondness for the job, as it is hard work and involves long hours, sometimes referred to as 'unsocial hours'.
- **Good social skills** An ability to communicate with other people in a friendly and polite manner. This includes colleagues as well as customers.
- **Initiative** An ability to see an opportunity and make the most of it in a positive way. This

may be simply reacting to a situation to avoid a customer's dissatisfaction by putting it right or enlisting support quickly, or providing good ideas for improving the quality of the service or product being offered.
- **Information technology skills** It is hard to come away from the fact that IT is used in virtually every part of leisure and tourism, so sound word processing, database and spreadsheet skills are vital to improve chances of good employment.
- **Knowledge of the product or service** No matter where you work you should be aware of what the company, office or agency is about. Brief yourself on every aspect, as you never know when you may be asked to cover, stand in for or even replace a colleague, or provide a service to customers – good knowledge gives confidence. Seize your opportunities – you never know, it may raise you up the ladder of progression. It certainly will not harm you or your future prospects.

As a guide, Figures 1.19–1.25 show typical progression routes in a selection of leisure and tourism areas.

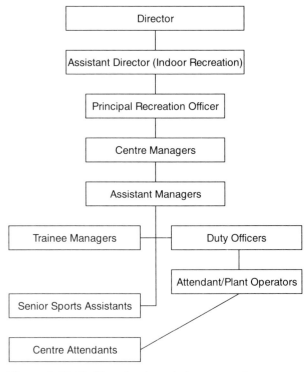

Figure 1.19 Staffing structure: indoor recreation

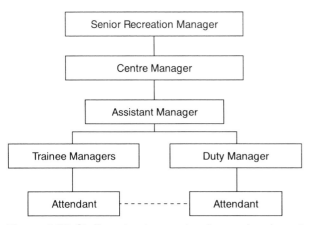

Figure 1.20 Staffing structure: swimming pool and sport and leisure centre

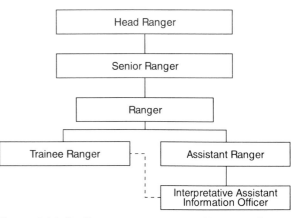

Figure 1.21 Staffing structure: countryside recreation

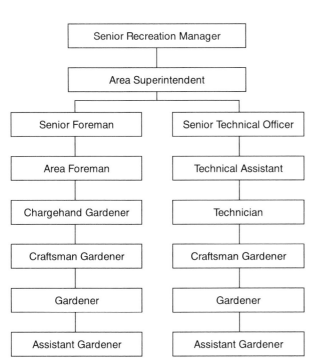

Figure 1.22 Staffing structure: parks and open spaces

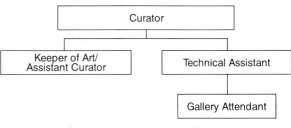

Figure 1.23 Staffing structure: art galleries and museums

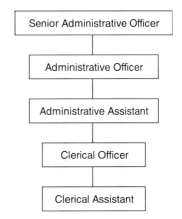

Figure 1.24 Staffing structure: local government – leisure and tourism

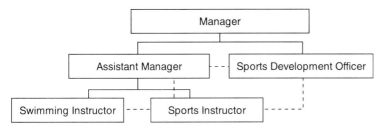

Figure 1.25 Staffing structure: sports instruction and coaching

Applying for a job

Writing a letter of application

A letter which supports a completed application form and accompanies a curriculum vitae has a different job to do from the letter which is the only submitted application document. The latter is sometimes requested as the sole means of written application and has to do the job all by itself:

'Interested applicants are invited to apply by letter to . . .'

In the first instance the main functions of the letter of application are:

- To formalize the act of application. Note the need always to refer to any enclosed documents – the application form and CV – to ensure they are not overlooked or misplaced.
- To act as a summary of what are considered the major strengths of the application. Bear in mind it does no harm to repeat them as a way of imprinting them on an employer's mind. He or she may be sifting through several dozen applications.
- To emphasize the applicant's suitability to this particular advertised post. Consider that the application form will have gathered the information the employer seeks and that the CV must of necessity be an all-purpose document to support an application for different types of job. The specific advertisement will have asked for particular qualities or abilities and the written letter provides a chance to demonstrate their possession – as far as the applicant is genuinely able to do so.

Good letters of application convey a sense of enthusiasm for gaining the advertised post without being either 'gushy' or swollen-headed in reciting accomplishments.

The letter of application should be kept fairly short – the equivalent of one side of A4 is suggested – and should be written by hand, firstly since this is still well established and secondly because employers like to get the feel of the application in personal terms. A few even submit handwriting for analysis, so this should sharpen up the scribblers among us!

The tone of the letter is properly formal and so 'Dear Sir' or 'Dear Madam' and 'Yours faithfully' are appropriate. While it is not always easy, avoid including too many 'I's in sentence constructions and particularly as the opening words of paragraphs. The British are a funny lot and the ability to blow one' s trumpet discreetly is expected in job applications!

Make sure you convey a sense of being readily available both for interview and to start the job if successful. It does not pay to suggest a starting date between the holiday needed after the stress of examinations and one's customary winter break!

ALWAYS take photocopies of *all* the documents despatched in support of a job application. If you are applying for lots of jobs you will find it otherwise impossible to recall what you wrote – and that is precisely what the interviewers will be scrutinizing in front of them when you are being interviewed!

NEVER send originals of examination certificates etc. with job applications. If employers are insistent, say you will bring them with you to any interview. Once lost, some may never be replaced in the same way, and their loss will cause much irritation and inconvenience.

Model letter of application

Dear Sir,

I should like to apply for the post of Assistant Leisure Centre Manager, as advertised in 'The Leisure Gazette' and have pleasure in enclosing my completed Application Form and copy of my Curriculum Vitae.

The advertised post particularly appeals to me, since my own career aspirations and education have been specifically directed for the last four years towards a management career in the field of Leisure Management.

In the fifth form of Roxborough School, I specialized in Business Studies and proceeded to Metropolitan College, where I undertook a GNVQ Leisure & Tourism Programme, leading to the Intermediate Level Diploma. On conclusion of this I progressed to the Advanced Level Programme, which specialized in Sport and Recreation, Leisure Management and related Business Studies.

I anticipate achieving a Merit grade pass at the end of my course.

During my full-time education I have undertaken work experience in a number of public and private leisure centres including: Roxborough Leisure Centre, Leisure World Pool & Spa and 'Physique' Health Club. This gave me an opportunity to gain valuable experience in the day-to-day management of leisure facilities. My placement reports were very good and are enclosed for your perusal.

If called I should be pleased to attend for an interview at any time convenient to you.

My course at Metropolitan College finishes on 30th June, 199_ and I should be available to commence a full-time appointment from the beginning of July onwards.

Yours faithfully,

Andrew Smith

The application form

The following information is generally required on an application form.

Name	
Address	
Telephone number	
Age	**Date of birth**
Status (whether married or single)	
Maiden name (if a married woman)	
Education	
Full time	
Part time	
Qualifications	
Current/previous	
Names and addresses of employers (if applicable)	
Details of employment – full, part-time work experience	
Outline of hobbies and interests	
Names and addresses of referees	
Date available	
Statement confirming as to accuracy of information supplied **Signature**	

The curriculum vitae

A curriculum vitae may be composed by using the following framework:

Personal details

- Full name and current address
- Telephone number
- Age, status – married/single
- Nationality
- Dependants – wife, husband, children (if applicable).

Education

- Secondary school(s)
- College(s) – with dates
- University – with dates
- Postgraduate institution
- Main subjects taken
- Activities, interests
- Post(s) of responsibility.

Qualifications

- Examination passes indicating grades, dates and examining boards.

Work experience

- Usually expressed by starting from the immediate past and working backwards
- Name of organization, location, job designation, range of duties, extent of responsibilities, reasons for leaving.

Interests

- Leisure activities, hobbies, indicating posts of responsibility – e.g. Honorary Secretary of Drama Club – where appropriate.

Circumstances

- Period of notice required to be given
- Mobility – car ownership, any limiting commitments.

A curriculum vitae is usually set out schematically, with appropriate dates and chronological structures.

Curriculum vitae – an example

Name	Andrew John Smith
Address	3, Southbank Drive Edgerton Smethurst PY1 1JF
Telephone Number	01804 165142
Age	18 Years
Date of Birth	8th August, 1977
Nationality	British

Education

Metropolitan College	1993 to present

BTEC GNVQ in Leisure and Tourism (Advanced Diploma)
Positions of responsibility:
   Student Representative
   Member of College Rugby team
   Member of Student's Committee

Roxborough High School	1988–1993

School Blue for Rugby	1993 to present

Positions of responsibility:
Prefect
Library Warden

Subjects Undertaken	Leisure Management
	Tourism
	Business Studies
	Sport & Recreation
	Modern Languages
	Information Technology

Qualifications

BTEC GNVQ	July 1994

Leisure & Tourism (Intermediate) Passed with Merit

NVQ Level 1 Sports & Recreation	July 1994
Six GCSE passes	June 1993 AEB
Mathematics	D
English Language	D
Geography	C
History	D
Information Technology	D
Art	D

Duke of Edinburgh Silver Award	June 1993
Community Sports Leaders Award	May 1993
ASA Bronze Award (Swimming)	March 1993
Duke of Edinburgh Bronze Award	November 1991

Work Experience

Roxborough Leisure Centre	July – August 1994

Assistant in Sports Hall. Preparation of racquets activities. Supervisor of game areas. Health and safety checks to game areas and changing rooms.

Physical Fitness Centre	February – March 1994

Work experience gained: circuit training, administration. Purchase and supply of fitness gear. Marketing of products.

Leisure World Pool & Spa	July – August 1993

Assistant in Leisure Pool and Spa. Preparation and cleanliness of all pool areas and changing rooms. Stocktaking of laundry area. Issue of keys and work log for clients. Safety reports to management. Ordering of vending supplies.

Interests
Leisure activities – rugby, swimming and cycling.

Circumstances
Present course concludes in July 199_
Car owner – full driving licence held

National record of achievement

Another method of presenting information to prospective employers is by way of the National Record of Achievement Log Books.

You are probably well aware of this and may be presently using them. Students undertaking courses in Colleges of Further Education may also be using the NRA documents or similar documents produced by the colleges themselves.

The following are typical examples of NRA material, but for reasons of space have been reduced in size.

Qualifications and credits

Subjects/qualifications, credits and awarding body	Level/results	Date achieved
Signature	Date	
Supported by	Position	

Personal details

Name
Date of birth
Address

Postcode

List of Secondary Schools, Colleges, Higher Education Institutions attended

Accreditation or validation, where applicable

Signature	Position	Date

College achievements

Curriculum

Provide brief particulars of achievement

Attendance rate

Signature (Teacher/tutor)

Signature	Position	Date

Other achievements and experiences

Signature	Date

Supported by	Position

Personal statement

Signature	Date

Employment history

Job titles and details   **Employer and address**

Signature	Date

Sources of information for careers and job vacancies

The following literature and/or contact points may help prospective new entrants into the leisure and tourism industry. Some specific careers may require contact with the organization directly. Only a selection is listed due to the space available.

Contact points

- Careers office run by the local council
- Careers tutor at school or college
- Local hotels and restaurants
- Local job centre
- Local leisure & tourism offices run by the council
- Local travel agencies

Literature

- *Leisure Opportunities*
- *Leisure Management*
- British Tourist Authority Publications on Careers
- *Travel Trade Gazette*
- *Caterer & Hotel Keeper (Careers Supplement)*

Information services

- Association of British Travel Agencies (ABTA)
- Business & Technician Education Council (BTEC)
- City & Guilds of London Institute (CGLI)
- English Heritage
- Forte Hotels
- Granada Leisure Group
- Institute of Leisure & Amenity Management
- Local libraries (college or school library)
- Mecca Leisure Group
- Rank Leisure
- The National Trust
- The Sports Council
- The Tourism Society

Reports are often produced by the government and leisure and tourism consultants. Copies of these may be available, such as:

- *Labour Intelligence Quarterly*
- *Labour Skills Report*
- *Working for Pleasure*

and many more.

These reports may sound very academic but often produce statistics which can help a new entrant in deciding a popular, specialist, or less popular career pathway in leisure and tourism.

Address directory

ABTA National Training Board
Waterloo House
11–17 Chertsey Road
Surrey GU21 5AL
Telephone 01483 727321/2/3
Fax 01483 756698

British Activity Holiday Association (BAHA)
22 Green Lane
Hersham
Surrey KT12 5HD
Telephone 01932 252994

British Association of Leisure Parks, Piers and Attractions (BALPPA)
25 King's Terrace
London NW1 0JP
Telephone 0171 383 7942
Fax 0171 383 7925

British Holiday and Home Parks Association
Chichester House
31 Park Road
Gloucester GL1 1LH
Telephone 01452 526911
Fax 01452 307226

British Tourist Authority (BTA)
Thames Tower
Black's Road
London W6 9EL
Telephone 0181 846 9000
Fax 0181 563 0302

British Travel Educational Trust
c/o 24 Grosvenor Gardens
London SW1W 0ET
Telephone 0181 846 9000
Fax 0181 563 0302

Business and Technology Education Council (BTEC)
Central House
Upper Woburn Place
London WC1H 0HH
Telephone 0171 413 8400
Fax 0171 387 6068

Camping and Outdoor Leisure Association (COLA)
Morritt House
58 Station Approach
South Ruislip
Middlesex HA4 6AS
Telephone 0181 842 1111/1292
Fax 0181 842 0090

City and Guilds of London Institute (CGLI)
76 Portland Place
London W1N 4AA
Telephone 0171 278 2468
Fax 0171 436 7630

Confederation of Tourism, Hotel and Catering Management
204 Barnett Wood Lane
Ashtead
Surrey KT21 2DB
Telephone 013722 78572
Fax 013722 77778

English Tourist Board (ETB)
Thames Tower
Black's Road
London W6 9EL
Telephone 0181 843 9000
Fax 0181 563 0302

Hotel, Catering and Institutional Management Association (HCIMA)
191 Trinity Road
London SW17 7HN
Telephone 0181 672 4251
Fax 0181 682 1707

Institute of Baths and Recreation Management (IBRM)
Giffard House
36–38 Sherrard Street
Melton Mowbray
Leicestershire LE13 1XJ
Telephone 01664 65531/2
Fax 01664 501155

Institute of Leisure and Amenity Management (ILAM)
ILAM House
Lower Basildon
Reading
Berkshire RG8 9NE
Telephone 01491 874222
Fax 01491 874059

Institute of Travel Agents (ITA)
113 Victoria Road
St Albans
Hertfordshire AL1 3TJ
Telephone 01727 54395
Fax 01727 47415

National Trust (NT)
26 Queen Anne's Gate
London SW1H 9AS
Telephone 0171 222 9251
Fax 0171 222 5097

Sports Council of England
16 Upper Woburn Place
London WC1H 0QP
Telephone 0171 388 1277
Fax 0171 383 5740

Tourism Society
26 Chapter Street
London SW1P 4ND
Telephone 0171 834 0461
Fax 0171 233 6551

Training and Enterprise Councils (TECs)
Central Contact:
The TEC Development Branch
TEED
Moorfoot
Sheffield S1 4PQ
Telephone 01742 753275
Fax 01742 758316

Training and Enterprise and Education Directorate (TEED)
Moorfoot
Sheffield S1 4PQ
Telephone 01742 753275
Fax 01742 758316

▪ Assignment 1.3 ▪

This assignment is made up of three parts:

Part 1
– A description of the principal job roles in different leisure and tourism contexts (see Glossary in GNVQ Unit handbook).
– Identification of job roles suitable for yourself.
– An explanation of the qualifications, skills and experience required for the job roles chosen.

Part 2
– An investigation on how to acquire the skills, qualifications and experience identified in your chosen job roles.
– An indication of the main sources of information on courses and job vacancies.
– A description of different ways of how to present personal information to possible employers.

Part 3
– Production of a personal curriculum vitae, suitable for submission to a possible employer.

Coverage of all three parts will be best conducted by undertaking a series of tasks which are listed in sequence, in order to help you.

Coverage

- Element 1.3
- Performance Criteria 1 to 7
- Core Skills opportunities
  Communications
  Information technology.

Task 1

After some research, provide a description of the principal job roles in a selection of leisure and tourism contexts (see Glossary in GNVQ Unit handbook).

This information may be best presented in the form of a table, e.g.

Job roles	Qualifications	Skills	Suitability

Indicate on the table suitable roles for yourself.

Task 2

- *Provide the qualifications, skills and experience of the job roles chosen and add them to your prepared table.*
- *On a separate sheet, indicate how you would acquire the qualifications, skills and experience necessary for the job roles you have chosen.*

Task 3

Produce a list of as many sources of information as you can think of for career advice, information and job vacancies within leisure and tourism. Provide addresses where known.

Task 4

Provide information on the different methods of how an applicant can present personal information in support of a job application.

Task 5

Provide a curriculum vitae for yourself for use in support of a job application. The curriculum vitae should be based on your present qualifications, skills and experience.

All your work should be word processed.

MARKETING AND PROMOTING LEISURE AND TOURISM PRODUCTS

Marketing and promotion

The marketing function

Marketing has been defined by the Chartered Institute of Marketing as:

> the management process responsible for identifying, anticipating and satisfying customer requirements, effectively and profitably.

The emphasis here is on satisfying customer requirements and needs, because satisfied customers will always come back – and in coming back hopefully the organization will continue to make profits.

Let's study the key words in the marketing definition:

- **Identifying** means finding out who exactly our customers are, what are their needs and wants.
- **Anticipating** means trying to forecast future needs and wants of the customer – anticipating customers' expectations and demand for a leisure product and service and making sure it is available (e.g. encouraging your retailers to stock up for Christmas, in good time for the increase in anticipated sales, or getting them to take in a new designer range of swimwear for the summer).
- **Satisfying** means providing products and services at a price and at a time and place which satisfy the needs and wants that have been identified.
- **Profitably** – all private organizations need to trade profitably in order to survive. For non-profit making organizations, for example

local authorities, voluntary bodies (libraries, colleges, museums, National Trust, etc.), the emphasis here would be on providing customer satisfaction as efficiently as possible.

The function of marketing is therefore everything to do in business which attracts and keeps customers. The role of marketing is concerned with getting the right product to the right customer at the right price and at the right place and time. It is not simply another

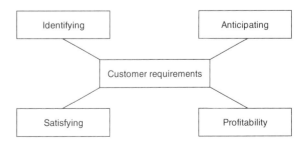

Figure 2.1 The marketing function

Figure 2.2

name for selling, nor is it simply about spending large sums of money on TV advertising campaigns. It is not only to do with junk mail which lands on your doorstep, offering incentives to buy, nor is it merely to do with marketing research. Marketing is in fact all these activities and more, enabling an organization to make decisions on what it will offer for sale, how much it will charge, who it will sell to and how it will deliver and persuade its customers to buy.

As a customer, however, we have choices. We can decide to buy or not to buy. To be successful an organization must therefore tailor a product or service so that their customers are satisfied, so that they prefer to choose and buy from us rather than going elsewhere.

Task 2.1

When you buy food you satisfy a basic need for hunger and thirst. Think carefully, however, about your other needs and wants, as a customer when you buy from:

- *Ice-cream van*
- *Fast food outlet (e.g. McDonald's)*
- *Restaurant*

1 *List your requirements as to what you expect before you will buy.*
2 *Compare your needs and wants for each of the above.*
Element 2.1, PC1

The marketing concept works on the principle that all business activities have customer implications. Everyone in an organization should therefore think 'customer' because without customers there would be no business.

Consider the following quote from *Mickey Mouse Marketing*, by N. W. Pope, on the success of the Walt Disney organization:

At Disney if your job is interfacing with the public (customers), in any way whatsoever, you are 'on stage'. If your work is not public interfacing you are 'backstage'. One is not better than the other. That is emphasized. There are no 'little insignificant jobs'. It takes many people, doing many types of jobs, 'to put on a show'.

The marketing mix

The marketing mix refers to the tools or ingredients of marketing – the activities which the organization uses to influence customer demand for its products and services. Think of a baker who, in having a recipe, needs the right balance of ingredients mixed in the right order and baked in the right way to satisfy different customer tastes. The skill lies not just in the baking, but in anticipating what your customers want or prefer and in satisfying their needs.

There are four ingredients to the marketing mix which are particularly relevant in satisfying customer needs. These are:

1 Product
2 Price
3 Place
4 Promotion.

These ingredients are often called the 4 Ps.

Product

It is only through products and services that customer needs are satisfied. A product or service is something people buy to satisfy a felt need. All organizations therefore must have products in order to bring in business. Most products are physical, such as tennis racquets, trainers, books or magazines, but services such as a haircut, concerts and holidays are also products (sometimes called service products).

The term product covers a wide range of goods and services. Below are a few examples of leisure and tourism products.

Figure 2.3

Goods	Services
Tennis racquet	Concert
Football shirt	Football match
Garden spade	Event
Leisure centre	5-a-side football session
Newspaper/magazine	Short break
Hotels	Package holidays
Theatre	Show
Theme park	Roller coaster ride

We can even think of persons and destinations as products, for example, the band 'Take That' can be marketed, not in a sense that we 'buy' them, but in the way we give them attention, we promote their records and organize their concerts. In effect the leisure product consists of a set of satisfactions which the organization delivers to the customer.

Go back to the first activity when you identified your needs and wants to buy an ice cream or a Big Mac or a meal in a restaurant. Did you identify several needs and wants you needed to satisfy before you purchased the product? These satisfactions can include quality of service, the standard of facilities, atmosphere, friendliness of staff, even image.

Figure 2.4

Case study

As a student you do not have a lot of money, but when the opportunity arose for you to see and hear your favourite band live at the local town hall, you could not let the chance slip by. Getting the money to pay for the ticket wasn't easy, but as you explain to your friends afterwards, it was well worth it to hear the group live. However, on reflection, the leisure experience was not altogether a success. The band's performance was great, but you were unimpressed by the manner in which you were greeted by the ushers, the poor service at the bar and the lack of comfort and visibility of the seating arrangements. Next time, you tell yourself, you will try somewhere else.

A product is made up of a variety of characteristics, or elements, all of which play an important role in providing a satisfying leisure experience. If one element falls short of what you expect, it can badly affect your satisfaction with the overall experience.

Task 2.2

In small groups identify and list the product/service characteristics you expect to find at a:

- *Nightclub*
- *Bowling alley*
- *Theme park.*

Element 2.1, PC1 and 2

Price

Price denotes the published terms on which the organization is willing to provide its product or service. All products and services incur costs, through payment of wages, materials and overheads. It is only through the prices it charges that an organization is able to cover its costs by generating revenue and thereby satisfying its own aims for profit or efficiency. However, organizations have to be aware of the value which customers place on their products and services, or, in other words, what they are willing to pay for them. Almost always there is a standard price for a product or service, but sometimes there are promotional prices offered to encourage customers to buy more of the product or to use a service at different times.

How price is used to attract customers

Pricing is a major reason why people do not participate in leisure and tourism experiences. Leisure and tourism organizations are well aware that some people are willing to pay more for a product or service, which others will only buy if the price is much less. For this reason, they do not set a single price, they set a price structure that covers different products and reflects variations in geographical demand, seasonal demand and customers. Some of the more common approaches to pricing differentiation are discussed below:

Geographical This is to do with deciding how to price its products to customers in different locations. British Rail often charge higher prices overall for long distances to reflect the higher transport costs incurred. However, in many locations, particularly in the south east of the country, the prices charged for journeys into London are disproportionately higher in respect of the distance travelled.

Price discounts Most leisure and tourism organizations may well modify the basic price for cash or early payment for volume purchases or bookings, and off-season buying.

- **Cash discounts** Most organizations will give cash or early payment discounts to encourage their customers to pay up as soon as possible.
- **Quantity discounts** A quantity discount is given to customers who buy in volume. Tour operators who buy hotel beds or airline seats often receive substantial discounts because of the numbers they buy.
- **Seasonal discounts** This type of discount is offered to customers who decide to buy the product out of season (e.g. take a holiday in Majorca in February or buy a swimwear outfit in the autumn). Ski manufacturers will often offer seasonal discounts to retailers in the spring and summer to encourage early ordering. Hotels, theme parks and airlines will offer seasonal discounts on their off-peak or slow selling times of the year.
- **Promotional pricing** This type of pricing is temporary and comes in several forms.
  Loss leader Supermarket and department stores often reduce their prices on well known brands in order to stimulate additional store-traffic (i.e. customers). The idea is you will come for the bargain but hopefully will buy something else.
  Leader pricing Also known as market penetration pricing leader pricing is designed to attract as many customers as possible to buy the product. Often used to stimulate demand for new products or services (e.g. airlines use this approach when starting up a service to a new destination).
  Cash rebates Customers are offered money-off coupons, air-miles, etc. to purchase the product or service within a set time period. This approach stimulates demand without costing the organization as much as cutting the price. The reason is many buyers fail to mail back the coupons for a refund.
- **Discriminating pricing** This is when the organization sells its products at two or more prices. Again there are several approaches.
  Customer segment pricing Here different customers are charged different prices for the same product, for example children,

students, unemployed adults, group, etc.

Image pricing   Here prices will vary dependent on the product's image. Leisure wear manufacturers often supply some retailers with the same product, except it may change the package or brand name. Customers will often pay more for the branded product than for the unbranded product.

Location pricing   Locations are often priced differently although the cost of offering each location is the same. Beer and spirits often cost more in town centres than they do in the suburbs. A theatre varies its seat prices according to its audience preferences as to where they want to sit (i.e. circle, stalls, box).

Timing   Here prices are varied by season, day or even hour. British Telecom varies its telephone charges in the day, at night and at weekends.

Task 2.3

Go to your local bus or train station and obtain a price list. Investigate differences in prices for particular geographical locations (or zones), times of the day, week. Suggest reasons for the price differences.
Element 2.1, PC1, 2 and 3

Place

Place is concerned with getting the right product to your customers at the right time. The leisure product or service will not be of much use to the customer if it isn't located where people expect to find it, or isn't made available when they want it.

Most services such as a game of squash, a football match, a concert are sold at the place where they are produced. However, most products are made some distance away from the place where customers want to buy them. The principal objective of place is therefore distributing the product to a place where the customer wants to buy it.

In achieving this objective, distribution of leisure and tourism products is concerned with:

- *Transportation*   ensuring the product is delivered to the right place at the right time.
- *Packaging and display*   trying to make the product more manageable in terms of the space it takes up in the shop, how it can be stored or displayed.
- *Stock holding*   ensuring there is sufficient stock of hotel beds, airline seats, tennis racquets, football boots available in readiness for when customers want to buy them.
- *Communication*   providing advice on availability of tickets for a large event, delays on arrival times or for handling complaints.

Not all leisure and tourism organizations have the finance or resources to provide all the above functions. An airline wanting to sell flights direct to the public would have to provide a network of shops in all the major cities in the UK and abroad in order to sell its flight tickets. It could sell direct by accepting bookings over the phone or through the mail, but is this the place where the customer wants to do business? Imagine each separate airline with its own distribution system – the cost of providing the tickets would be extremely high and would duplicate the retailing effort.

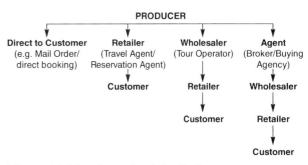

Figure 2.5 The channels of distribution

Although some products are sold direct, the majority pass through a chain of intermediary organizations who deliver the product to the customer. Figure 2.5 highlights the key distribution channels involved.

If we use the example of an airline once again, then the airline is the producer of a transport product or seat. The airline can sell its seats in a number of ways.

1 *Direct to the customers* possibly at the airport or by direct booking at its offices.
2 *Through a retailer* 70–80 per cent of airline seats are sold at travel agents.
3 *Via a wholesaler* large numbers of airline seats are sold to tour operators who in turn use these seats to create package tours.
4 *Via an agent* Agents or airbrokers often purchase large numbers of seats at bulk prices on behalf of several smaller tour operators so as to share the risk of not selling all the seats.

Task 2.4

In groups consider what distribution channels could be chosen by leisure and tourism producers to sell the following:

● *Hotels in seaside towns with empty rooms available for letting*
● *Unbooked theatre seats*
● *Packaged holidays abroad*
● *Cruises on the Norfolk Broads.*

Individually consider the role played by the following in the distribution of leisure and tourism services.

● *Reservation agency*
● *Travel agent*
● *Tour operator.*
Element 2.1, PC1 and 2

Location plays a major part in the success of leisure and tourism. Consider how many more people would be able to use the National Art Gallery in London if it could be transported around the country at dates and times to suit all. Leisure and tourism providers very often rely on customers visiting their locations. However, where there is a large range of leisure products or activities available in a location, such as a town centre, leisure complex or shopping area, people will be prepared to travel several miles to it.

Task 2.5

In small groups, examine the following leisure organizations and decide where best to locate them, giving reasons why:

● *Tour operator*
● *Further Education college*
● *International hotel*
● *Travel agent specializing in exotic holidays/business trips*
● *Theme park.*

Some possible choices of location are: town/city centre; edge of town; countryside; suburb, near major motorways/airports; location not important.
Element 2.1, PC1 and 2

Choosing the wrong location can be a serious error for many tourism and leisure organizations. Think of the costs of building a new hotel, a swimming pool or a new football stadium. These facilities cost many millions of pounds. We need to attract lots of customers over many years if we are to make any profits.

Task 2.6

Some commentators believe the choice of location for Eurodisney, just south of Paris, was the wrong location.

1 Do you agree? Give reasons why.

2 Suggest an alternative location for Eurodisney, giving reasons why.

Promotion

Promotion is concerned with telling our customers about our products and services, in the hope of influencing their perceptions and behaviour. In simple terms, people are unlikely to buy our products or services if they have never heard of them.

Needless to say, we cannot promote our services until the product, price and place have been sorted out first. When they are, it is important to use promotion to attract our customers by creating a favourable image of what our organization and its products can do for them.

Task 2.7

Consider the leisure products and services below and decide how you would go about telling potential customers about them:

● The Grand National (horse race meeting)
● New nightclub
● Packaged holiday abroad
● Local derby football match.

The need for market research is explained

To ensure that customers receive satisfaction from their products, leisure organizations must acquire sufficient information on their customers to understand their needs. Without this information organizations are unlikely to offer their customers the best mix of products, price, place and promotion.

Marketing research is the means by which an organization obtains information about its customers. The information it obtains is necessary in giving marketing decisions on planning the marketing mix.

Case study

The Sinclair C5 electric motor vehicle, although a technological wonder for its day, is an example of a product which was launched without any marketing research having been carried out. It failed. However, it is probably less significant than the fact that the product had been designed without a customer in mind. This is evident from Figure 2.6.

Figure 2.6

This does not mean that all businesses need to spend large sums of money on formal marketing research projects. It does mean, however, that all leisure providers must recognize that their customers are constantly changing in terms of age, occupation, income, marital status and that needs, wants and even tastes and values of these people need to be monitored in some way.

Main types of information

There are two basic sources from which information (i.e. data) can be obtained:

- Secondary source
- Primary source

Secondary – Secondary information is data which has been produced for another purpose, but may be relevant to our understanding of customer needs. For example, in any organization there are sales returns on what is bought, by whom, in what quantity. The accounts departments have figures on prices charged and revenues obtained. Secondary data can be obtained or purchased from external sources such as government (HMSO), commercial organizations, libraries or research agencies:

- *Internal sources*
  Membership lists
  Accounting files
  Gate receipts
  Visitor records
- *External sources*
  Census data
  General Household Survey
  Commerical organizations
  Trade directories/associations
  Research agencies/panels.

Primary – When the information you seek is not available from secondary sources it may be necessary to conduct some primary or field research. An example of primary research is a survey using questionnaires to study business travellers' current attitudes towards other

Figure 2.7

airlines competing on the same route. Alternatively, it could simply mean the manager of one travel agent monitoring (i.e. observing) what competing travel agents are offering in terms of choice of holiday or any special deals:

- Surveys
- Observations.

Clearly the more we know about our customers, their needs, what interests them, the easier it is to create, promote and deliver our service profitably, to the satisfaction of the customer.

Target markets and how to divide into market segments

The word 'market' has been defined as a place where buyers and sellers meet to trade. This word tends to suggests some large collection of people who may be interested in the product or service your organization is offering. Those who can be identified as being interested are your potential market, and those who buy are your actual market or customers.

Offering your product or service to everyone pre-supposes everyone is interested in your product and will receive some benefit or satisfaction from it. Not everyone wants to go swimming, to play football, or relax on a beach. However, there will be groups of people who will take part in the same leisure or tourism activity or who may find benefit from buying our type of product, and it is to these groups of people we should target our offering.

People buy things to satisfy their needs, but people often buy the same thing for different reasons. The young teenagers may go to the swimming baths for fun, the parents take their children to learn to swim, while the swimming club use the same swimming baths because they can obtain certain days, reduced rates for their club members to train. A person's needs and wants closely affect the reasons why they buy different products and services.

Building up a profile of their customers, helps organizations to divide up their markets and so better understand what it is their customers want. For example, various models of car, records, fashion products often tell us something about the type of people who buy them. Think of the products or services you use which reflects on your personality. They may include clothes, the way you cut your hair, the holidays you take.

Marketing professionals have long recognized that few organizations have products or services that can attract everyone successfully. Can you think of any?

Task 2.8

Imagine you are a manager of a sports centre involved in programming the leisure activities for the main sports hall. Popular as it may be, would you offer football only sessions in the main hall or would there be other activities you would wish to offer?

1 Identify any other activities and draw up a profile of the customers who you think would want to use them.
2 How might the needs and the profiles of these customers differ from those of the footballers.
Element 2.1, PC1 and 4

As can be seen from the task above there are very often sub-groups to your market who have different needs and as such why not offer these sub-groups different products or services. Dividing markets into sub-groups or segments is a process called market segmentation.

How to segment markets

There are five basic methods of segmenting your markets or customers. These methods enable organizations to build up profiles of their customers.

- *Demographic* This is to do with dividing an organization's customers by age, sex, marital status, or ethnic group.
- *Geographic* This covers where customers come from. Whether they are from the north or south, or whether they live in urban or rural areas etc.
- *Socio-economic* This describes groups of customers who share common characteristics of income, social class, occupation, even levels of education. Below is a set of characteristics by social class.

| GRADE | DESCRIPTION | |
	General	Services
A	'Upper-middle class' Higher managerial, administrative or professional – has demand for 'quality' and luxury products as well as 'normal' requirements – may be trend-setter too.	Good demand for banking, investment; better grade hotel and restaurant; more expensive tours and independent travel probably with 'special' interests (music, art, archaeology, etc.).
B	'Middle class' Middle to senior management and administration; up and coming professional – often likes to be trend-setter. Requires most products	Usually has need for investment and banking; probably strong interest in insurance as means of saving as well as protection; good middle grade hotels etc.; more adventurous tours and group travel.
C1	'Lower-middle class' Junior management, supervisory and clerical grades. Tends to ape the trend-setters even if finances overstretched.	Minimal use of banking and investment services; insurance for protection and some 'compulsory' saving; probably 3-star hotel and restaurants; packaged tours but could also have special interests (music, art, etc.).
C2	'Skilled working class' Usually a manual trade. Requires the less costly products usually.	Limited banking (current account); some protective insurance; 2- and if possible 3-star hotels, etc.; packaged tours (could also have special hobbies/interests).
D	'Working class' Semi- and unskilled worker. Mainly interested in the least expensive products.	Very limited use of banking and insurance; probably 2- and 1-star hotels etc.; one holiday a year, if abroad the cheaper package and probably Spain. Could still have special interests.
E	Pensioners and widows.	Minimal demand, if any, for all services.

Figure 2.8 Classifying the consumer by social class

● *Geo-demographic* This method combines demographic and geographic factors of segmentation. The most common method used is a computerized database called ACORN (A Classification of Residential Neighbourhoods). The idea behind this method is that people who live in certain residential type areas often share similar values or beliefs, buy similar products, go on similar holidays. If you accept this idea, then by identifying where your existing customers live (the postcode will do) and processing the data through the ACORN database you can:
  • Profile your customers by household residential type
  • Locate potential customers of similar profiles and interests throughout the country.
● *Lifestyle* This method divides customers up by culture, attitudes, even personality types. One of the best lifestyle ways of classifying customers is by assessing their needs through the life of the family. Called the Family Life Cycle it assesses the needs of the customer over nine life stages. These are depicted in Figure 2.9.

Stages in the family life cycle

---

1 Bachelor stage: young single people living at home

2 Newly married couples: young, no children

3 Full nest 1: youngest child under six

4 Full nest 2: youngest child six or over

5 Full nest 3: older married couples with dependent children

6 Empty nest 1: older married couples, no children at home, head of household still in the workforce

7 Empty nest 2: older married couples, no children living at home, head of household retired

8 Solitary survivor in the workforce

9 Solitary survivor, retired

Adapted from Wells, W. D. and Gubar, G. (1966) 'Lifecycle concepts in marketing research', *The Journal of Marketing Research*.

Figure 2.9 The family lifecycle

Task 2.9

1 Identify at which stages in the life cycle you, your brothers or sisters, parents or even grandparents are.
2 Try and work out for yourselves in broad terms the leisure and travel opportunities likely to appeal to people at each of the nine stages.

Element 2.1, PC1, 4 and 5

How the marketing mix relates to target markets and market segmentation

Segmentation within leisure and tourism can be done on different levels.

● The industry can be segmented by activities such as tourism entertainment, heritage, sports, art, etc.
● Sports can be segmented into indoor and outdoor sports.
● Outdoor sports can be further segmented by type of sport (e.g. football, cricket, hockey, running, etc.).
● Football can be segmented by type of supporters (e.g. children, adults, families, disabled, etc.).

The great advantage of this marketing technique is it focuses the organization into identifying exactly which markets and what needs it intends to satisfy. It helps the organization refine its marketing mix, for example, a leisure pool facility may consider whether it is more profitable or efficient to offer swimming facilities for mother and toddlers (segment) during certain times of the day rather than have the baths open to the general public. It may choose to operate special events (e.g. swimming gala) in order to attract other market segments. In effect, the organization uses segmentation to target its customers.

In the 1950s large firms like Coca-Cola and Butlins made lots of money by selling large quantities of one or two standardized products or services to mass markets, using promotional methods such as television. Now things have changed in the market place – because of increasing competition people have more choice. Coca-Cola today make caffeine-free, diet, cherry and other types of coke and soft drinks. Butlins now offer a choice of Leisure Worlds in the UK and abroad where there is a vast variety of attractions, accommodation, meals and entertainment to choose from. We could see these changes as an increase in the variety of products offered, or we could see it as an attempt by these organizations to match their customer needs more precisely by developing products for different market segments and to maintain their custom.

Different segments of the market may need different amounts of money spent on them to ensure the benefits offered by the product or service meets the needs of the target segment. Consider, for example, one-off events at a leisure centre, a field and track event, a swimming gala or a basket ball tournament. These activities tend to appeal to very specific types of people and as such are sub-sectors of a market for sport. Profiling the types of customers and their needs through segmentation analysis allows the leisure centre to make fine adjustments to the product/service, the price it charges, when to hold the event, even the type of promotional literature to put out to attract these customers. It is a fact that customers respond better to offerings that are tailored and aimed directly at them rather than to broader type.

As a tour operator you could for example decide to cater for groups of holidaymakers according to their age, social class, or even where they live. Let's assume you have decided to develop specialist packaged holidays for customers living in particular parts of the UK. You might want to feature as benefits to these groups, the convenience of local airport departures, free car parking at the airport as well as courtesy bus services. You may not be carrying as many customers as tour operators providing more mass appeal holidays to the whole of the UK, but you may find your customers are willing to pay a higher price for the added value of the services you have provided.

Task 2.10

1 In small groups, identify specialist holidays which are offered to particular groups of people and try and draw up profiles of the customers likely to buy these holidays.
2 List the features of the marketing mix (i.e. the types of product or services offered, the prices charged, the places or times at which they are made available and how organizations try to promote the holidays) for each of the specialized holidays identified.
Element 2.1, PC1, 4 and 5

Task 2.11

During the 1990s the 25–44 age group will increase as a proportion of the total population. What business opportunities is this change likely to bring for the leisure products below.

1 Fashion wear
2 Holidays
3 Going out to clubs/pubs
4 Watching TV.

Make notes on the opportunities (or threats) for a class discussion.
Element 2.1, PC1, 4 and 5

▪ Assignment 2.1 ▪

As part of a group you are to investigate the marketing operations of three sports centres, each offering similar leisure activities. More specifically you are to choose one sports activity (i.e. swimming, squash, badminton, 5-a-side, etc.) and examine how that particular activity is marketed by the sports centres. The findings from each of the sports centres is to be compared, highlighting any particular strengths and weaknesses and where appropriate making recommendations.

Coverage

- Element 2.1
- Performance criteria 1 to 5
- Core skills opportunities
  Applications of numbers
  Communication
  Managing self and others
  Information technology.

Task 1

Form a group of 3–6 members and decide on the three sports centres and the activity you wish to investigate at each site. Split the group into three sub-groups and decide which sports centre each will investigate.

Task 2

Find names and addresses for each sports centre and identify any contact names (e.g. General Manager, Assistant Manager, Publicity/ Promotion Officer). Plan visit.

Task 3

Individually or in groups of two visit the sports centre and observe how it is marketed, making notes under the following headings:

- Place   *The location of the sports centre should be plotted using a local map of the area. Information will be required to be obtained and plotted such as the position of the organization relative to the nearest town, or within the town. You should also note its proximity to transport systems, physical features, car parking and nearest competitors.*

- Product   *Identify when the activity chosen is available at each sports centre through the week, including casual use, leagues, competitions, social events. Using graph paper draw a plan of the centre to scale, showing where the activity is available. Leave a space at the side of the plan to make a list of all complementary services on offer, such as sauna, bar, restaurant, viewing gallery, creche, car parking.*

- Price   *Obtain a list of prices (or membership fees) for attending the sports centre and taking part in the activity. Note any different concessionary rates for youngsters or OAPs etc.*

- Promotion   *Identify the types of promotion used by the sports centre. Where possible arrange to obtain copies of advertisements, leaflets, brochures, posters, etc., which will help give you some idea of the different groups of people (target markets) the sports centre is trying to attract to use/try the activity through the day/week.*

Task 4

Decide what other information you would like to have on how the organization is marketed which you may not be able to obtain simply by visiting the facility. Plan a series of questions that you can use when interviewing a staff member of the facility to help you identify the target markets for the activity. For example:

Who plays the activity?
When is the activity played?
Who else could take part in the activity?
Are there spectators involved?

Task 5

Carry out an interview with the Leisure Manager. You can do this by making a personal visit to the sports centre, writing a letter and/or by telephoning. (Note: The interview should be arranged at the start of the assignment although the actual interview should not take place until the study of the facility is complete).

Task 6

All group members should meet to share and review the information on each sports centre investigated. An analysis of the target markets for the activity and the marketing mix needed to promote the activity should be described and compared.

Task 7

The group must now decide how best to present all the information on how the activity has been marketed at all three sites. The information is to be displayed and the group are to provide an informal presentation on the sports centres investigated.

Promotional campaigns

Different types of promotion

However good a product, it will seldom sell itself. Knowledge about the product has to be communicated. Promotion is about communicating knowledge between one person or organization and another person or organization.

There are several basic forms of communication which leisure and tourism organizations use:

- Advertising
- Public relations (PR)
- Sponsorship
- Display
- Selling
- Direct marketing
- Sales promotion.

Advertising

Each year leisure organizations such as Granada Leisure plc promote their leisure products and services using advertising. The advertising is often targeted at consumers (i.e. the general public), but it can also be targeted at the trade (i.e. tour operators, reservation agencies, travel agents etc.). The channels and advertising media they use may include TV, commercial radio, national newspapers, magazines, poster sites, buses, and even trains. Small leisure and tourism organizations also use advertising, but may use local media services such as local newspapers.

Public relations

This form of promotion is to do with marketing an organization's image. It can be divided into *press relations or publicity* and *non-press relations*. Leisure organizations use publicity in order to get free editorial press coverage, in news stories about themselves. Non-press relations are used to promote an organizational image via open days, exhibitions, providing prizes, charity events and sports days, etc.

Editorial coverage can be carried in all forms of media such as newspapers, magazines, radio or even TV. Think of the number of times in a TV news bulletin or 'chat show' that pop stars, company products, even politicians get a mention. Although a lot of people are sceptical about what they are told in advertisements, they often believe a story they read in a newspaper, hear on the radio or watch on TV – which makes PR a very persuasive form of communication.

Sponsorship

Sponsorship is about giving money to support some organization or event in exchange for which the sponsor usually gains some free advertising or public relations coverage. This is a growing area of promotional activity in which the leisure and tourism industry, particularly sports, does extremely well.

Some examples of sponsorship include:

Sponsorship	*Sponsors*
Round the World Yacht Race	Whitbread
Football League	Endsleigh Insurance
British Library	Digital Equipment Co.
Rugby World Cup Series	Famous Grouse Whisky
Professional Tour of Britain	Kellogs

The main reasons why companies are willing to invest many thousands, sometimes millions of pounds into a sponsorship deal is to do with building a favourable image with its target markets. The activities they sponsor are invariably well supported and followed with interest by their markets, and by association it is believed their markets will become interested in the sponsor, its products or simply gain a favourable awareness for the name.

Task 2.12

Below are some of the UK's top sports sponsorships and sponsors

Mars	Tennis
Embassy	Football League
Milk	Darts
Benson & Hedges	London Marathon
Martell Brandy	Formula One Racing Cars
Malboro	Snooker
Embassy	Darts
Robinsons	Cricket
Rothmans	Cycling
Barclays	Grand National

Can you identify which sponsors sponsored which sports.
Element 2.1, PC2

Display

If you want your products to be seen you have to put them on display. Display, like exhibitions, is about drawing attention to your product by making it stand out at the point of sale.

Display is often used to promote certain products, for example, a new line of leisure wear, a prestigious holiday or possibly old stock such as sale items. Some shops have corporate display policies where counters all have open-ended tops and merchandise is displayed in the same way. The reason for this is to create an image of reliability and trust which is visible by the store being instantly recognizable to its customers.

Selling

Selling is about talking to individuals or small groups of people. It includes face-to-face selling between, for example, tour operators and travel agents or between travel agents and the public. It is an extremely powerful way of communicating and persuading people to buy, but very costly for this reason. Where personal contact is involved the target market is often very small. Each unit of that market can be made to feel he or she is being approached as an individual.

Remember, selling is about helping people to buy rather than selling them something they do not want.

Direct marketing

Direct marketing, like selling, is another means of talking directly to your customers. Unlike selling which is face to face, direct marketing uses the telephone or the mail to communicate with much larger numbers of people. With the growth of computerization many companies, large and small, have found this method of promotion to be very cost effective in communicating with its target markets.

Companies build up lists of customer names from a variety of sources which they believe will have some interest in their products, for example, from:

- Sales receipts bearing the names and addresses of past customers
- Responses to advertisements for their products
- Membership lists, annuals or directories
- Hiring or buying other organizations' lists (i.e. list brokers).

Whether by phone or mail the target market is the mailing list. Today, direct mail takes third place behind press and television in the promotion stakes and up to 10 per cent of the total UK expenditure on advertising.

Sales promotion

Sales promotion is to do with making people an offering, for example 'visit our restaurant this weekend and receive a weekend break accommodation voucher' or 'buy four cinema tickets and get 20 per cent off'. The emphasis is on getting people to buy now rather than later. Sales promotion comes in many forms but the most commonly used offers include:

- *Price reduction* – sales offer, e.g. 10 per cent off your summer holiday if you book early.
- *Coupon* – money off your next purchase.
- *Free product* – 'two for the price of one' offer at a restaurant.
- *Trading stamps* – free air miles when you use your credit card to book your reservation.

Task 2.13

1 *Provide other examples of sales promotion offers other than those listed above.*
2 *Look through last month's back copies of local newspapers and identify stories about:*

– *your favourite football club*
– *the area in which you live or go to school.*

Compare the amount of coverage in each case and the topics written about. Decide overall whether the publicity gained was good or bad.
Element 2.1, PC1 and 2

Use of media

The term 'media' is used in marketing to mean the various channels of communication used in advertising. A single channel is called a medium. The more common advertising media used by the leisure and tourism industry include TV, radio, cinemas, newspapers, magazines, outdoor posters, point of sale and brochures.

Television

Most people in the UK have access to a television. It is estimated that 98 per cent of all households in the UK have at least one set and the majority have two, most of which are colour televisions. Advertising can only be offered on independent television such as ITV or Sky Television and in selected regions on cable television. ITV covers 13 regions in the UK and offers advertisers the choice of regional or national advertising. Sky Television, together with Good Morning Television (GMTV) and Channel 4, offer national advertising.

TV advertisements can be as short as a few seconds, or longer. ITV rates for advertising vary from region to region and from hour to hour. Prime viewing time is normally from 6.00 pm to 10.00 pm each evening.

Task 2.14

The rates charged for two independent television regions, Border and London Weekend Television, are given in Figure 2.11.

1 *Compare how much a 30 second advert costs for each region at 12.00 am midday, 6.30 pm and 10.00 pm in the evening.*
2 *Suggest reasons why the rates for one region are much greater than the other, and why they are higher and lower at different times of the day.*
   Element 2.1, PC2
   Element 2.2, PC3

Commercial radio

At the time of writing there are 83 licences representing approximately 120 commercial radio stations covering the UK. Audiences are predominantly young people, housewives and people driving to and from work. Customer profiles differ from region to region, but females outnumber male listeners.

The cost of advertising on radio is far less than on TV, but, like TV, rates vary by region and from hour to hour. Unfortunately for the industry, most businesses which advertise nationally continue to use TV so most advertising on radio comes from local advertisers.

Cinema

Cinema offers advertisers all the sound and colour of television, plus a larger screen. However, gone are the days of the 2000 plus seated cinemas. Most cinemas today are multiplex cinemas providing seats for a few hundred people per screening. Advertising is usually concentrated at the start of the showing of a film. Audiences tend to be in the 16–24 age group, people on dates or young married couples. These people generally have money to spend, so advertising tends to concentrate on items such as cosmetics, cars, confectionery, soft drinks, holidays and fashionwear.

Video cassette recorders (VCR)

Most of us have seen advertisements on the video cassettes we hire promoting new film releases on behalf of the film distributors. Some advertisers also offer videos about their new products and services. Disneyworld in Florida often advertises its attractions in the national press encouraging you to send for their promotional video. Tourist boards, hotel groups and others will supply promotional videos to travel agents, to airlines or coach operators as a way of encouraging their customers to stay at their hotel or visit their holiday destination.

MAP OF ITV AREAS

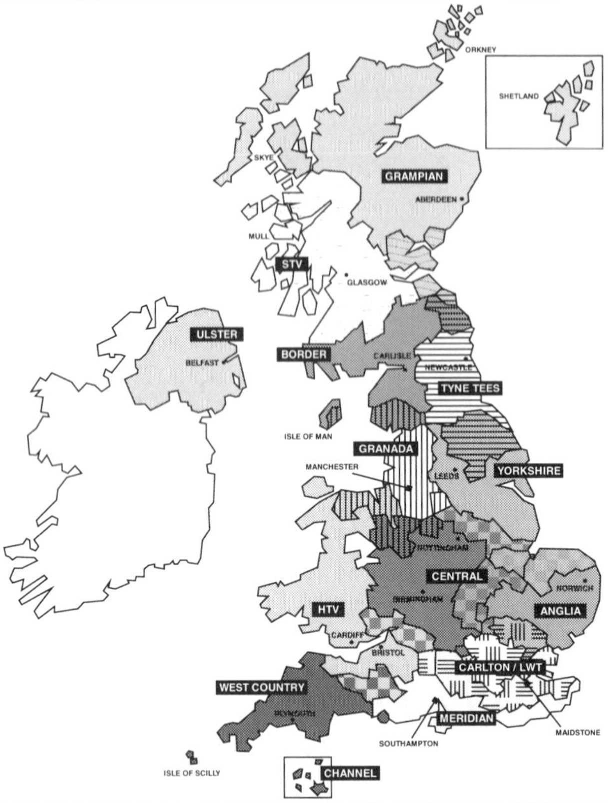

NET ITV INDIVIDUALS

	'000s	%
CARLTON/LWT	10,786	19.32
CENTRAL	8,769	15.70
GRANADA	6,532	11.70
YORKSHIRE	5,427	9.72
TYNE TEES	2,754	4.93
STV	3,521	6.30
GRAMPIAN	1,157	2.07
HTV	4,223	7.56
MERIDIAN/CHANNEL	5,161	9.24
ANGLIA	3,733	6.69
WESTCOUNTRY	1,571	2.81
ULSTER	1,551	2.78
BORDER	654	1.17
	55,839	100.00

Source: Jul 92 - June 94 BARB Establishment Survey/ITV Estimates

Produced with acknowledgement to BARB

Figure 2.10 Map of ITV areas (courtesy of BARB)

Television Standard Rates
RATES CARDS

London Weekend Television

Code	10"	20"	30"	40"	50"	60"
R3	£30,000	40,000	50,000	66,665	83,330	1,000,000
R2	15,000	20,000	25,000	33,333	41,665	50,000
R1	5,000	6,666	8,333	11,110	13,888	16,666

Border Television

Code	10"	20"	30"	40"	50"	60"
R3	£18,000	24,000	30,000	40,000	50,000	60,000
R2	9,000	12,000	15,000	20,000	25,000	30,000
R1	3,000	4,000	5,000	6,666	8,333	10,000

TV Segments

Code	Time
1	up to 17:15
2	17:16 – 19:30
3	19:31 – 23:30

Note: The above rates are not fixed and can fluctuate depending on the television programmes being viewed, the type of audience the programme attracts as well as the type of advertiser wishing to book a particular TV slot.

Figure 2.11 Standard television rates (courtesy of Laser)

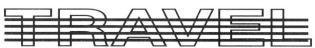

Figure 2.12a Display ad (courtesy of United Norwest Travel)

Cinemas and Theatres

 **MULTISCREEN**

NONSUCH LEISURE PARK

ANYLANE, NEWTOWN ROAD
SOMERSET

 ACCESS/VISA HOTLINE 0123 456 789
24 HOUR MOVIE INFORMATION
0123 456 456

BARGAIN SHOWS DAILY BEFORE 7.00PM
WHEELCHAIR ACCESS TO ALL SCREENS

Children's Entertainment

BOUNCY CASTLES

Bouncy Castles £20.00
Weekend Special 1111 555 555

Public Houses

THE JAZZ BAR

AT THE MANSION COUNTRY CLUB

SOME ROAD, SOMELEIGH, WENTWAY   TEL: 1234 777 888

☆ *Wentway's Only Purpose Built Jazz Bar & Lounge*
☆ *Fully Air Conditioned with Comfortable Seating*
☆ *Supper Menu and Coffee Available*
☆ *Late bar until 1am Friday & Saturday* ☆

FRIDAY NIGHT - RHYTHM & BLUES

Taxis and Mini-Cabs

DICKS CHAUFFEUR SERVICE

24 hour airport service available
All airports covered
Heathrow single £20. Return £35
Courier Service also avilable

Telephone: 8888 999 000

Figure 2.12b Classified ads

Newspapers

The British are avid newspaper readers. Newspapers are provided nationally and locally, daily and weekly, giving Britain probably the best coverage of newspapers anywhere in the world. The total average daily sale of newspapers in 1990 was approximately 15 million copies.

The major circulation of newspapers is in the tabloid press. Circulation and readership often determine the rates that are charged. However, in addition to the national press there is a much larger number of regional and local newspapers, the majority of local being free newspapers (i.e. you don't pay for it).

Basically two types of ads can be placed in newspapers (see Figure 2.12):

- *Display ads* – these adverts are generally bigger and much more expensive. They are placed amongst news stories so that they stand out and get noticed.
- *Classified ads* – these adverts are normally a few lines of copy listed under category headings. They are also the life blood of local newspapers.

Magazines

There are many types of magazines which differ quite a lot in terms of size, appearance and who they are aimed at. The most common types are:

- *General* These are produced mainly on a monthly basis. The magazines are aimed at the mass markets although they generally cater for women (e.g. *Nova, Cosmopolitan, Woman, Prima, She).*
- *Specialist magazines* There has been tremendous growth in the development and sales of these magazines, particularly in the hobby and leisure areas such as photography, home computers, DIY, gardening, holidays and sports.

- *Retail trade* These magazines are provided for businesses and include the *Travel Trade Gazette*, the *Grocer, Hotel & Catering*. Advertisers tend to be producers wishing to inform retailers of their new products and services.
- *Professional* Most professional associations have their own monthly or quarterly publications. The majority are circulated by post to their members rather than sold in shops.

Task 2.15

Visit your local newsagent in groups of four and note all the magazines on display. Analyse them under the categories discussed above and any sub-categories you think appropriate, such as leisure, travel, computers, DIY, etc.

Element 2.2, PC5

Outdoor posters

Outdoor advertising is probably a better term for a wide variety of media used, including posters, hoardings, flashing signs, bus and train adverts. Most if not all of this type of advertising is aimed at attracting attention so as to remind people of a product or to reinforce a more detailed TV or newspaper message.

Point of sale

Point of sale includes a variety of media including shelf-talkers, mobiles, wire stands, illuminated displays, banners, stickers, flags, all of which are designed to attract our attention and direct the customer's eye at a particular message. The medium is very often placed directly above the product it is referring to and positioned at a point where most people decide to look, try or buy.

Brochures

Brochures come in many sizes and forms, mostly in colour. In the case of tour operators, the brochure represents the product offering in a tangible form. It spells out in print and through colour what the tour operator's products and services consist of. The brochure allows the company's product to be displayed on shelves and to be taken home. One of the questions often faced in leisure and tourism is whether to produce different brochures (or leaflets) for different market segments. It is for this reason you can obtain travel brochures on trains, ferries, and bus services, and separate brochures on short or long break holidays using the same travel services, but offering accommodation and services, possibly under holiday destination headings.

Aims and objectives of promotional campaigns

The main purpose of promotion for the leisure and tourism industry is about communicating messages about its products and services. Telling customers what they have to offer and persuading them to buy from us rather than go elsewhere.

The message has three main purposes (known as the 3As) and are designed to:

1 Make customers *aware* of new products or services.
2 Provide information in order to change *attitudes* or reinforce a customer's views or perceptions of the product or service.
3 Encourage customers to take *action* (i.e. to visit a facility).

Customers are unlikely to buy from you if they are not aware of the products and services you have on offer. Attracting their attention is an important first step in communicating with your customers. Having got their attention you now need to gain customer interest for your message. This is crucial in persuading them you have what they want and in forming and altering attitudes towards your organization. The type of message and how it is presented must appeal to your customers if they are to take any action, such as to apply for a brochure on your ferry services or better still book a trip on one your ferries.

The purpose of promotion is to generate movement of customers towards some action. The type of action it seeks should ultimately lead to increased sales, greater use of a facility or, in the case of the theatre more 'bums on seats'.

Task 2.16

Individually or in groups look at the four advertisements in Figure 2.13, aimed at promoting the leisure industry.

1 List and compare the purposes of each of the four advertisements.
2 Do you think the advertisements achieved their apparent purpose? Give your reasons?

Element 2.2, PC3
Element 2.3, PC3

Case study

Four national tourist boards (NTBs) have been set up to promote tourism throughout Great Britain. These are the English Tourist Board (ETB), the Scottish Tourist Board (STB), the Wales Tourist Board (WTB) and the Northern Ireland Tourist Board (NITB). Their job is to provide information to persuade the domestic tourist to visit their areas of the country. They do this by providing promotional leaflets and brochures on different tourist destinations and events and are supported in their efforts by a number of local area and regional tourist boards.

The British Tourist Authority (BTA) was set up in 1969 to oversee the national Tourist Boards and to act as an umbrella organization for consolidating their efforts when promoting the UK abroad. How the BTA does this is by having sales offices in many countries abroad including, for example, USA, Germany, France, Austria, Saudi Arabia, Australia and Ireland. These offices consolidate and distribute the promotional leaflets and brochures of the national and regional tourist boards across the UK. In addition they liaise with overseas travel agents and tour operators by organizing seminars, exhibitions and travel trade shows.

A very effective way of promoting the UK is to invite overseas journalists and travel trade customers to visit various parts of the UK on what is called familiarization trips. Although coordinated by the BTA very often it is the national and regional tourist boards and their public and private sector partners, who are engaged in leisure and tourism, who actually provide the accommodation, travel arrangements, catering and entertainment. The major benefits obtained from this arrangement are that it provides enormous scope for the facilities that can be offered and is a way of sharing the cost of the trips. Similarly the BTA will sponsor stand space at the world's largest tourism exhibitions such as the World Travel Market London, ITB Berlin and MITCAR Paris, at which the authority will share space and costs with its partners.

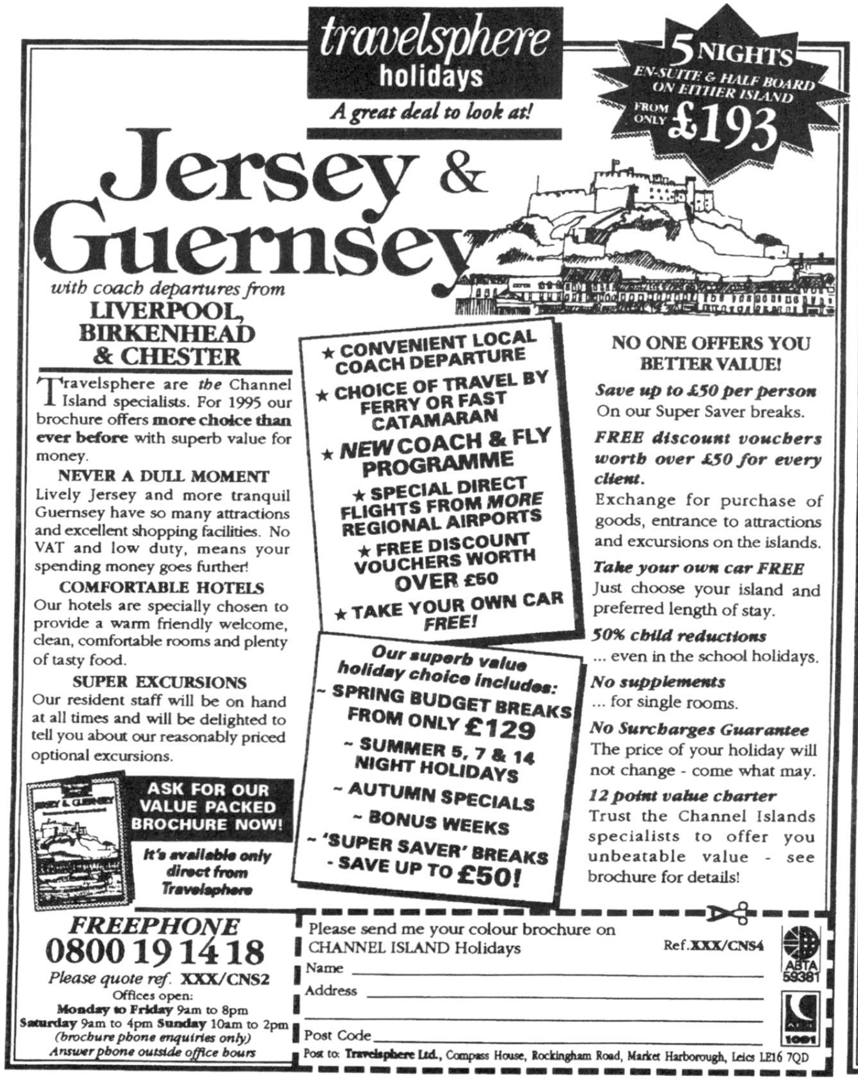

Figure 2.13(a) Courtesy of Travelsphere Ltd.

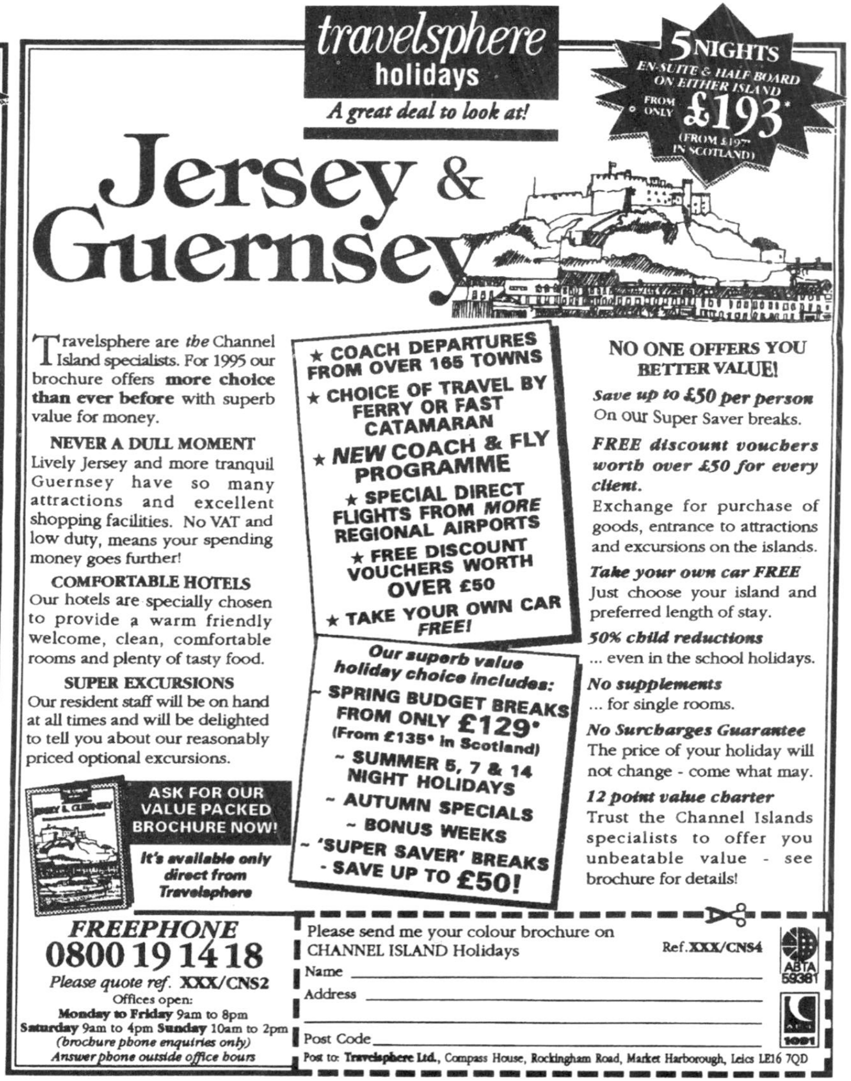

(b) Courtesy of Travelsphere Ltd.

Figure 2.13(c) Continued

GREAT ATTRACTIONS THAT MAKE YOUR DAY

1. **BACKSTAGE TOUR** – see what's behind your favourite programmes. **(30 MINS)**
2. **SOUNDSTAGE TOUR** – see the famous sets come to life. **(30 MINS)**
3. **THE BAKER STREET VICTORIAN EXTRAVAGANZA.**
4. **THE CORONATION ST. EXPERIENCE** – programme history and the hallowed cobbles. **(CONTINUOUS)**
5. **SOUND EFFECTS SHOW. (30 MINS)**
6. **THE HILARIOUS HOUSE OF COMMONS DEBATE. (30 MINS)**
7. **THE SOOTY SHOW. (30 MINS)**
8. **DOWNTOWN NEW YORK.**
9. **UFO ZONE** – a nail biting voyage into an alien spacecraft. **(CONTINUOUS RIDES)**

BRAND NEW FOR '95

10. **ROBOCOP: THE RIDE** – a thrilling new experience on MotionMaster, our futuristic computer simulator ride. **(CONTINUOUS RIDES)**
11. **HAUNTS OF THE OLDE COUNTRY** – European premiere of a truly spooky 3-D show. **(APPROX 20 MINS)**
12. **3-D ROCK LASER SHOW** – a spectacular 3-dimensional high powered laser display accompanied by great rock tunes. **(15 MINS)**
13. **DEADLY EFFECTS** – gory special effects straight from the horror movies. **(30 MINS)**
14. **CORONATION STREET STUDIO SETS** – famous interior sets and a Street Star appearance on site every day.

Figure 2.13(d) Granada Studios tour literature

Special Facilities.

We hope the following information will assist your movement around the site and enable you to visit every attraction. Should you need any further assistance please do not hesitate to contact any member of staff.

TOILETS
Disabled facilities are situated in the following areas:
New York Street
Exhibition Hall, upper level
Stables Restaurant, Grape Street
Deerstalker Pub, Baker Street

LIFTS
A lift is situated inside the New York De Vere Hotel, for access to upper level.

SHOWS
There is disabled access to all shows on site, as follows:–

UFO Zone:	Via entrance ramp on Grape Street.
MotionMaster:	Although this attraction cannot be ridden by disabled guests, the film may be viewed from a stationary position.
The Sooty Show:	In New York Projections, disabled access via ramp.
House of Commons/ 3D Show:	Via lift in entrance of De Vere Hotel, up to Exhibition Hall.
Sound Effects Show/ Make-Up Show:	Situated on ground level.

Access Coronation Street via lift in New York De Vere Hotel and through Baker Street set.

EXIT
When you are ready to leave the grounds please make your way to the main entrance gate, which will be opened for you.

BABY CHANGING
New York Street
Stables Restaurant, Grape Street
Rovers Return Pub

TELEPHONES
New York Street
Coronation Street
Rovers Return Pub

PHOTOGRAPHY
Photography of the Tour is encouraged. Free camera hire courtesy of Kodak is available from Laughing Stock on New York Street. Films are sold in all our shops.

Task 2.17

1 Review the promotion activities of the BTA and decide which of these activities are primarily concerned with:

a making visitors aware of new tourism products/services in the UK.

b providing information to alter (or reinforce) visitors attitudes or perceptions of the UK.

c encouraging visitors to visit the UK.

Give your reasons why.

2 What would you consider to be the main advantages and disadvantages for a domestic tourist taking a holiday in the UK? If you were the marketing manager for ETB how would you go about promoting these advantages to the residents of the UK?

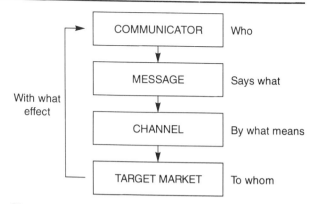

Figure 2.14 The communication process

Promotional campaigns are about sending messages to potential customers through various channels or media in order to create awareness and understanding as to why they may wish to buy a particular product or service. Leisure organizations in this context are the senders of the message and target market customers are the receivers of the message.

Figure 2.14 explains the process by which an organization communicates with its target market.

The process of communication starts with the source of information or communicator, i.e. the leisure or tourism organization with a message to deliver. The leisure organization must determine what message to deliver to its target market, in order to create awareness and understanding. Euro Tunnel for example, may have different messages it wants to send to the different target markets it serves. To the

business market segment the purpose of the message may be to communicate details of its high speed links with European cities, or informing them of its unique roll-up-and-run train schedules. The leisure market segment may be more interested to hear about new low prices in the main holiday periods.

If there are lots of facts to communicate to the customers such as train schedules, different holiday destinations and accommodation, you will probably need to have the message printed. However, if you are trying to inform a large market of customers as to when the new train service will begin, or to get them to use it quickly, some form of advertising and/or sales promotion may be more appropriate. The kind of message you want to send and the target market you want to receive it will determine the form and the type of media channel most suited to delivering it. Campaign objectives must therefore relate to the promotional techniques most likely to achieve them

Some of the more common campaign objectives are given in Figure 2.15.

How organizations use promotion is dependent on what they want to achieve. Some organizations use promotion to build for the future, while others use it to generate business today. Promotion techniques such as display, selling and sales promotion are clearly intended to get customers to act/buy sooner rather than later.

Advertising	PR
1 To create awareness for or to remind people about a tourist destination	1 To attract more investment in the leisure and tourism facility locally
2 To encourage more people to visit a region/facility	2 To bring public attention to some conservation problems such as pollution on the beaches
3 To create or stimulate desire for a new product	3 To create a favourable image of the facility's services

Sales promotion	Selling
1 To improve brochure display and maintain stock levels	1 To improve sales of a product
2 To increase sales in off-peak times	2 To obtain more effective displays for your products in retail outlets
3 To increase membership numbers quickly	3 To maintain jobs in the leisure industry

Figure 2.15 Campaign objectives

Watching a commercial on TV, reading stories in newspapers or having a 'chat show' guest on radio talk about a new play they are working on at a local theatre, may not have an immediate impact in attracting customers. It attracts our attention and in the long run may build a favourable image of the theatre as a place for, say, new more livelier productions. In the future when you think about going to watch a play you could decide to go to your local theatre rather than going elsewhere.

When setting the aims and objectives of a promotional campaign leisure and tourism organizations need to be clear as what it is they want to achieve and the promotional technique or mix of techniques that will be most effective.

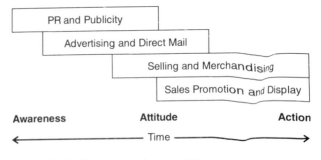

Figure 2.16 The persuasion process

Some promotional techniques may be designed to achieve all three stages in the persuasion process at the same time, others will simply seek to gain attention, while some will focus on action by getting people to buy now.

Figure 2.16 is a guide to the overlapping effect that most promotional techniques obtain in achieving one or more of the expected objectives given above.

PR, publicity and advertising are seen as good techniques for providing information and making people aware of the products and services available. Advertising and direct mail should also be seen as suitable mediums for altering attitudes and images people have of our products and services. Selling, sales promotion and display, on the other hand, while having an effect on attitudes are clearly focused on getting people to take some form of action (e.g. to visit a destination or buy a product).

Case study

Leisure centres are traditionally quiet during the day and busy in the evenings. Many more staff are therefore required in the evenings than through the day to look after visitors, but because of the shortened hours are often only offered part-time employment. Part-time workers, by the nature of their work, are not always as well trained as full-time staff.

A leisure centre may wish as a primary objective to increase the number of full-time sports and recreational employees so as to enable it to offer a greater variety of sport disciplines to a wider range of people. In order to do this the leisure centre may decide to run a promotional campaign to increase the usage of the facility by spreading its customers throughout the whole day.

Task 2.18

Try and think of ways in which the leisure centre above could encourage greater use of the facility in the daytime and so meet the primary objective to provide for more full-time skilled staff.

Element 2.2, PC3 and 4

Key factors affecting the success of a campaign

Offering 50 per cent off a skiing holiday may be an effective means of promoting a ski resort to tourists, but only if the message is directed at people who can and want to ski and can afford the time and money to pay for it. How many of you would be tempted to go to sunny Spain in the winter despite a 50 per cent reduction on summer prices.

How we deliver our message, in what form and how often, are also very important questions we need to get right if we are to be successful. Should we use advertising on TV, in national newspapers or on radio? How about promoting our message via exhibitions, posters or window displays in travel agents, specialist winter holiday brochures or via a combination of some or all of these promotional tools?

Huge sums of money are spent by organizations such as Alton Towers, British Airways, hotel groups like Truste House Forte and tour operators such as Thompson Holidays promoting their tourism services – many of these organizations spend millions of pounds – too much to gamble.

To be successful therefore requires the organization to ask several questions about its promotional campaign, for example:

- *Awareness* – does it attract attention, does it inform, does it raise awareness?
- *Attitude* – does it improve or enhance the image of the leisure product or the organization? Does it provoke interest in the product or does it maintain or reinforce a favourable perception of the product?
- *Action* – does it make people apply for a brochure? Does it increase sales or does it attract new customers?

There are many factors which can affect the success of a promotional campaign. Several of the more common factors are listed below:

- Marketing research
- Target markets
- Market knowledge and perceptions
- Media selection
- Competition/distraction
- Costs
- Budgets
- Timing
- Legal and ethical constraints
- Professional/design skills.

Marketing research

Marketing research is often used by leisure and tourism organizations to help them decide what form or mix of promotion is best for their product or destination. By observing who is attracted to a leisure facility and by asking people why they chose this facility not another helps organizations to decide the right mix of promotional techniques to use. Researching secondary sources of information in libraries can also prove very useful.

Libraries have a tremendous amount of secondary information about the amount of leisure time or disposable income different groups of people have available to them, how they spend their time and money on different types of products and leisure activities. They also have lots of information about the media which may be useful to organizations wishing to get across a campaign message to its target market. For example, Benn's Media Directory provides details about TV and radio companies, newspapers and magazines. British Rate and Data (BRAD) provides a comprehensive coverage of virtually all media that sell advertising space in the UK, together with their rates.

Target markets

The campaign objectives of a leisure organization should clearly state what market it wants to communicate with, since precise targeting of its messages can save money and ensure an effective response.

Market here refers to the ultimate user of the product or service and as such must be described in terms of their numbers by age, gender, social class, location, etc. For example, a local theatre may decide its next musical production would be highly suited to groups of young adults between the ages of 20–34. However, with over 13 million people in the UK within this age bracket, the theatre will need to be more precise in its targeting. By considering its location, in relation to its local population or the catchment area from which it expects to attract customers, the theatre will help define the boundaries in terms of how far and how many people the campaign needs to cover. You may also wish to consider the social class of those people to be covered, their income levels and gender. Most theatres recognize that generally 50 per cent more females visit the theatre than males. This can help in the selection of media to us – its format and design of the most appropriate message to obtain a response from the targeted audience.

Table 2.1 illustrates population age changes from 1971 to 2031 (projected).

Table 2.1 Population (in thousands) 1971–2031 (Source: *General Household Survey*, 1989, HMSO)

	1971	1976	1981	1986	1988 Base	1991	1996	2001	2011	2021	2031
Persons all ages	55,927	56,216	56,352	56,763	57,065	57,533	58,462	59,201	59,989	60,823	61,200
0–4	4553	3721	3455	3642	3747	3914	4136	3973	3594	3837	3740
5–9	4684	4483	3677	3467	3619	3656	3918	4140	3686	3708	3852
10–14	4232	4693	4470	3690	3394	3484	3666	3928	3987	3610	3844
15–19	3862	4244	4735	4479	4250	3707	3499	3681	4164	3712	3722
20–24	4282	3881	4284	4784	4728	4496	3724	3517	3960	4019	3628
25–29	3686	4239	3828	4237	4495	4746	4469	3700	3675	4157	3721
30–34	3284	3629	4182	3787	3892	4200	4702	4430	3458	3899	3972
35–39	3187	3225	3589	4158	3847	3771	4170	4669	3643	3619	4099
40–44	3325	3136	3185	3561	4005	4132	3742	4133	4379	3420	3858
45–49	3532	3262	3090	3142	3209	3518	4079	3691	4585	3586	3566
50–54	3304	3423	3179	3023	3055	3080	3450	3997	4014	4265	3333
55–59	3365	3151	3271	3055	3000	2919	2980	3339	3519	4389	3433
60–64	3222	3131	2935	3055	2940	2873	2756	2817	3681	3719	3956
65–69	2736	2851	2801	2641	2865	2759	2614	2516	2913	3091	3867
70–74	2029	2260	2393	2364	2166	2267	2379	2272	2263	2988	3041
75–79	1356	1499	1708	1837	1860	1853	1816	1920	1798	2118	2259
80–84	803	849	968	1132	1196	1265	1306	1313	1354	1374	1825
85+	485	538	602	709	796	894	1056	1166	1315	1313	1484

Task 2.19

1 Briefly describe the trends in age structure indicating which age groups are continuing to increase and which are continuing to decrease.

2 Describe the effect these trends may have on the planning for leisure and tourism provisions.

Element 2.1, PC1
Element 2.2, PC4

Market knowledge and perceptions

In order to design and communicate the right message to one target market, it is important to have a very clear idea about the market's knowledge or awareness of our organization and its products, and their attitudes towards them. The sorts of questions the leisure and tourism organizations must ask, include:

- What proportion of the market is aware of who we are, the leisure products we produce, our holiday destinations and what they can offer?
- What image of the organization do our customers have?
- What image or beliefs about the organization or its products do we need to change?

Over time people build up perceptions and images of an organization, its products and services based on what they know or think they know. These perceptions can be based on experience or can simply be formed from reading an article about a leisure organization in the press, talking to friends, etc. Right or wrong a person's perceptions are real to them. By understanding what our market knows or perceives about our organization or products can help us best decide what messages to send to them.

Some leisure organizations often take a short term view about promotional campaigns. They believe the creation of an image to be academic

or only suitable for very large companies, while promoting the lowest price message offers the greatest chance of success. This is far from true. While no one would deny the need at times for this type of promotional activity many more far sighted organizations will often seek to obtain publicity or place regular advertisements in the local or national press. This approach may be used to draw the attention of its markets to the variety and choice of its service, on the professionalism of its staff, in providing advice or as a way of altering or reinforcing attitudes towards the leisure organization.

Media selection

The choice of media is wide, from national and local press, TV and radio to magazines, directories/guides, direct marketing and posters, etc. Which media to use is often determined by what:

1 The campaign objectives set out to achieve.
2 The number and geographical spread of the organization's target markets.
3 What it can afford.

If the objectives of a promotional campaign are to attract the attention of a very large number of people across the country – possibly to make them aware of a new holiday destination – then the choice of national television and/or press may well prove most suitable. However, if the objectives are simply to attract increased use of the sports hall at the local leisure centre, then advertisements placed in local press or use of the local radio or direct mailing of promotional leaflets may be more appropriate.

Competition/distraction

No one will be interested in your facility or tourist destination, if they have never heard of it – so gaining the attention of your target market is vital if you are to create interest and ultimate action. Most of us, however, are exposed to thousands of hopeful messages every day from hundreds of organizations all trying to promote their products and services.

Messages on the radio as you eat breakfast, on posters as you wait for the train, in the newspaper as you read during your journey to work, through an evening telephone call from a friend about a nightclub opening shortly, and on television as you try and relax before going to bed. The competition creates so much distraction we have to accept that our target audience/market will never absorb all the message one campaign puts out. Worse still, most of our target audience will never ever notice it, and of those who do, only a few will remember if for any length of time.

Costs

That television is an effective medium is obvious. Equally understood is the fact it is extremely expensive. The costs of advertising on national or even regional television can be prohibitive except for the very largest of leisure and tourism organizations. Besides the screening costs, there is also the cost of producing the advertisements. Not surprisingly, having produced a TV advertising campaign most organizations seek to use it frequently, particularly at the peak times when your target audience is likely to be watching.

Inevitably it all comes down to what the organization can afford i.e. what budget is available.

Budget

The amount of money budgeted for a promotional campaign can restrict the type of promotional techniques to those that can be afforded. It can also restrict the length and frequency of the campaign, which in turn reduces the coverage or number of times your message can be delivered to your target market.

Ensuring adequate coverage of your market audience so that most have the opportunity to see (OTS) your message can cost a lot of money. A thirty second advertisement on national TV together with its production can cost many thousands of pounds. A long nationwide campaign including TV and press coverage, posters, brochures, etc. could cost millions of pounds. All organizations have a limited amount of money they can afford to spend on a promotional campaign. Most leisure and tourism organizations do not have the resources available to afford national press or TV promotions. Many of course have no need of such expensive media since their target audience may well be local to them. Nevertheless, before any campaign can be designed and planned it must take into account the budget available.

Timing

If you had an unlimited budget you might wish to run your promotional campaign through the year. Inevitably, most organizations cannot afford this, so organizations have to decide when is the most appropriate time to communicate their message.

Most media can carry messages in a very short space of time. Local papers and commercial radio will accept prepared advertising copy twenty-four hours before publication. However, in the case of national magazines including Sunday supplements, bookings sometimes have to be placed several weeks in advance of the publication coming out, and where television is concerned, advertisement bookings often have to be placed many months in advance, particularly for a large campaign.

Legal and ethical constraints

All organizations should be aware of legal and ethical constraints on their campaigns. The Advertising Standards Authority (ASA) set down rules for the promotion of goods and services. Also, the law requires that all offers are truthful, and that organizations only make promises which they can deliver on.

Professional/design skills

Most promotional activities require lots of specialized skill in planning and preparing campaigns (e.g. from carrying out marketing research, generating ideas, preparing copy lines, visuals, and logos, to preparing press releases and buying media space). Most leisure organizations do not have all those skills in-house and so are restricted to what they can do and what they can afford others to do for them.

Tour operators and travel companies traditionally publish their holiday travel brochures well before Christmas for the next summer season. A lot of effort is spent by their salesforces getting the travel agents to distribute their brochures offering trade incentives based on future sales. After Christmas the tour operators will spend a lot of money on PR and in advertising nationally on TV and in the press to alert the public to their products and to get them to visit the travel agents and pick up one of their brochures. To advertise before Christmas is unlikely to have the desired impact on diverting attention away from Christmas itself.

Task 2.20

As manager for a toy manufacturer you are planning a promotional campaign to promote a new toy for Christmas.

In groups decide when would be the best time to:

1 sell the toy into retail shops
2 advertise the toy to the general public.

In answering the above, you should indicate when to begin and for how long the campaign should run giving your reason why.
Element 2.2, PC3 and 4

Case study

Most people in the UK have access to a television. Advertising on independent television can cost huge sums of money, yet in 1992 the BBC Channels attracted over 50 per cent of all TV viewers. Worse still a national survey in 1990 found nearly 20 million adults in the UK sometimes missed seeing ads even when screened at peak viewing hours, while 4 million adults in the UK skipped viewing ads almost always.

Task 2.21

Individually identify the TV programmes you normally watch. Note the times of the day through the week. List the programmes shown under ITV and those under BBC.

1 Can you recall any particular ads shown at the time of the TV programmes? If so list them.
2 State what you can remember about one of the ads (its message, what it wanted you to do, how you felt about it).
3 How successful was it in raising your awareness of its products or services, altering your perceptions or in getting you to take some action?
Element 2.2, PC3

▪ Assignment 2.2 ▪

Individually, or in pairs, you are to investigate the product(s) of several tourism organizations, their prices and markets. Five holiday products are to be investigated. You can choose the products from a selection of brochures which will be provided for you. It is important to ensure that the holidays chosen are from different organizations and will appeal to different groups of people in order to provide choice. You may, however, wish to choose holidays you yourself are familiar with.

Coverage of performance criteria and range for Element 2.2 is built into the assignment for Element 2.3.

Task 1

Choose five different holiday brochures to investigate.

Task 2

Examine the nature of each of the holidays on offer in terms of characteristics and features.

Task 3

Determine who the likely target markets are for each of the five holiday products. Try and provide customer target profiles (e.g. age, gender, social class and family, etc.), for each of the holidays.

Task 4

Plot the variations in price for each of the five holidays: for example high, low, medium seasons, group/individual prices.

Task 5

Carry out a survey to determine which holidays appeal to different groups of people and compare to the target profiles in Task 3. List the product features that appeal to each target group giving reasons why and identify any improvements that could be made to the holiday product.

Task 6

Collect all the information together and with visuals from the brochures individually write a report using a word processor which describes:

- *the nature of the leisure and tourism product*
- *the markets for which the products have been developed*
- *how pricing is used to attract the targeted market segments.*

Note: *The details of your analysis, including copies of your questionnaire, could be included as an appendix to your report.*

Planning, preparing, implementing and evaluating a promotional campaign

The campaign stages

Having agreed the organization's objectives and likely outcomes there are five basic stages in setting up a campaign. These are shown in Figure 2.17.

1 Market research	Initial research is required to establish the target audience and to provide clear profiles on each of the target groups to be reached. Further research can help with planning the messages and in selecting the most appropriate media.
2 Planning	Selecting the most effective promotional mix to reach and persuade the target audience to respond. Also involves deciding on how the campaign is to be developed and by whom, (i.e. in-house or agency). Deciding when and for how long the campaign should run and determining the budget to support the campaign.
3 Preparation	Briefing agency personnel to creatively design messages to meet the objectives. This involves copy writing, illustrations, logos, artwork, etc.
4 Implementation	Scheduling the chosen media, and determining coverage frequency and impact of the message.
5 Evaluation	Measuring the results of the campaign to see if our objectives have been achieved.

Figure 2.17 A five-stage approach to planning a promotional campaign

Determining the promotional mix

In preparing for a promotional campaign one of the key questions an organization has to ask itself is, how does it get its message across to its market.

Consider your own personal communications – when do you send a letter or make a telephone call rather than calling on someone in person? How do you decide which is the best way to get your message across? The same problem faces leisure and tourism organizations when deciding between the promotional techniques of:

- Advertising
- Publicity
- Sales promotion
- Selling.

If there are only a small number of people to contact, then maybe a sales call is best. For getting your message across to very large numbers of people advertising using the mass media may be required.

Selling, while expensive, is very good at getting people to buy a product. Sales promotion is also very good at influencing a purchase, particularly if you are seeking to get someone to try a product for the first time. It can also be used effectively to encourage repeat purchases, such as 'buy one and get 50 per cent off your next purchase'.

Advertising is excellent at creating awareness of and interest in a product which is always important when launching a new product or when reinforcing favourable beliefs. Where it is less effective is in getting people to act or buy the product. To adapt on old cliche, advertising can lead the public to view, but it cannot necessarily get them to buy. Not surprisingly, most promotional campaigns use two or more promotion techniques to get their message across.

When deciding which promotional techniques to use in a campaign, it is helpful to be aware of some of the advantages and disadvantages of each, see Table 2.2.

Table 2.2 Some advantages and disadvantages of promotional techniques

Promotional technique	Advantages	Disadvantages
Selling	Interactive & responsive Greater product acceptance Increases sales Builds buyer/customer relationships Good for targeting customers	Limited target audience Expensive
Sales promotion	Increases sales quickly Establishes purchasing patterns Helps move slow selling items (i.e. off-peak)	Provides little information No investment in long term sales Little brand building
Publicity	Message is very believable Increases awareness Customer investment	No control on what message is delivered Cannot guarantee the message reaching target audience May not be seen/heard
Advertising	Can reach large numbers of people Good at attracting attention and building awareness for a product Arouses interest Can target its customer	Message needs to be repeated several times to to be heard/seen Costs can be very high Can be very wasteful where message is sent to large numbers of people not interested in the product

Planning promotional campaigns for targeted customer segments

Customers are not all the same. It is also interesting to note that in many leisure and tourism industries there is a high percentage of repeat bookings or visits made by a small proportion of customers. This is known as the 80/20 rule or Pareto Effect. It simply means that it is usual for a small number of customers to account for a large proportion of the business.

Consider Figure 2.18. Here customers are categorized A, B or C according to the proportion of sales they account for. The A customers, perhaps 20 per cent of the market, account for 80 per cent of total sales. B customers, say 55 per cent of the market, account for 15 per cent of total sales, while C customers, representing 25 per cent of the market, account for only 5 per cent of total sales.

The holiday market relies heavily on repeat bookings year after year by customers who have acquired a taste or liking for a particular destination. In short, those people who have enjoyed their leisure experience will want to repeat their experience again and again.

By identifying those customers or potential customers who provide the largest sales, managers in the leisure and tourism industries

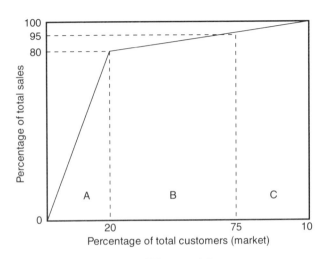

Figure 2.18 The Pareto Effect model

are in a position to develop messages that should have a good chance of success, rather than just developing a message on a hunch!

In this case, they will focus on reminding their customers of the things they enjoyed, highlighting the things that satisfied them, with the objective of encouraging repeat sales.

Case study

Giggleswick Leisure Centre has commissioned a marketing research study on who uses or could use their facilities during the off-peak times of the day. Part of the research findings has identified and classified the leisure centre's customers or potential customers into the following segments:

- Single
- Married
- Old
- Young
- Male
- Female
- Abled
- Disabled
- Employed
- Unemployed
- Local visitors
- Distant visitors (5 miles or more).

By drawing up a simple matrix of users (potential users) of the facility, the leisure organization was able to look more closely at such segments:

Age band	0–10	11–18	19–34	34–35	35–49	50–64	65+
Single							
Married							
Male				x			
Female							
Abled				x			
Disabled							
Employed							
Unemployed				x			
Local visitors							
Distant visitors				x			

The matrix identified the main user (potential user) as a married, able, unemployed man, between the ages of 35 and 49 who lives outside the immediate residential area of the leisure centre. Therefore, the management will have to consider customer characteristics of this segment in terms of:

- Excess free time
- Very limited income
- Possibly tied to looking after children while mother is at work
- Lack of self-esteem from being unemployed.

Task 2.22

The centre's squash courts are under-utilized for most afternoons, as is the swimming pool. Therefore, having identified and characterized the target market segment, as manager of Giggleswick Leisure Centre, design a promotional campaign aimed at attracting greater use of the squash court facilities and swimming pool in the afternoon from the target market segment.

1 Determine the objectives of the campaign.
2 Describe the message you would want to put across to encourage the target market to respond.
3 What promotional techniques do you think would be most effective from the point of view of cost and in reaching your audience? State your reasons.

Element 2.1, PC5
Element 2.2, PC2, 3 and 4
Element 2.3, PC2

The advertising agency

If you had to provide a new keep-fit programme for your local leisure centre or tell your customers about the new late night opening times you could well decide to place a small ad in your local paper or have some leaflets or posters designed and produced at a local print-shop – in effect do it yourself. However, if the items for sale require you to communicate with a very large target audience, it may mean having to produce a major holiday brochure, a TV or radio commercial or a colour advertisement in a national magazine. In this case, it is usual for leisure and tourism organizations to go to an advertising agency who have all the necessary skills and expertise to handle all aspects of the promotional campaign.

Most advertising agencies will provide the creative ideas to turn your promotional objectives into reality by preparing text, designing the layout of your brochures, leaflets, advertisements, preparing artwork, illustrations, photography, press releases and by producing commercials. They will arrange for materials to be printed and will purchase space in magazines and newspapers or purchase time on TV or radio so that your messages are carried to your audiences at the right time.

- *Account executive* Most agencies will appoint an account executive (or director) to look after your account and it is through this person that the creative teams of the agency will be briefed as to what you want from your campaign. The account executive is expected to understand fully the needs of the client in the context of its operations and industry and to interpret this back to the agency. When the campaign is complete the account executive will supervise the presentation of the agency's proposals to the client. The other agency personnel involved include:
- *Campaign planner* Sometimes this is the same person as the account executive. This campaign planner assists the account

executive and uses specialized market research to assess the target market characteristics, what they know etc. in helping to determine the overall campaign objectives and the message to get across. The planner will also test or evaluate the effectiveness of the campaign to see how the market has responded.
- *Media buyer* This person buys advertising 'space' in newspapers, magazines or 'air time' on TV or radio. The media buyer with the campaign planner researches and decides the type of media to carry and deliver the particular message.
- *Creative team* This may consist of an art director who will create and develop drawings or illustrations called *visuals* and a copywriter who will produce the words and straplines known as *copy*.

Preparing the promotional material

Creating the message

Selecting the agency to manage your promotional campaigns is like selecting a company to build an extension to your house. You will need to obtain quotations from several agencies to find out how much they charge. As with builders, the agency will need to visit you to get a clear idea of what you expect from the campaign (i.e. your objectives) and who you wish to communicate with (your target market). You will need to determine whether they have the expertise and resources to carry out all or part of your campaign. This is best achieved by asking for a list of their clients to see if they have any experience of dealing with similar businesses. It is also helpful to view some examples of their work to check it is of a standard of quality and creative design you would expect, or are looking for. Better still, let them make a presentation to you on some aspect or part of a campaign you are considering. Financially, you need to determine whether they can, or are willing to work to the budget you have agreed for the campaign.

Briefing the agency

However big or small your agency is, when providing materials for advertising, sales promotion, direct mail, PR, etc., there are a number of things the agency need to be briefed on in order to ensure that your organization's money is well spent and its objectives achieved:

- The nature of the leisure or tourism business you operate
- How the business has developed
- The marketing aims of the organization in general and the specific objectives of the promotional campaign
- The target audience; those people you want the promotion to reach and affect
- The budget for the work.

Having decided on the promotional objectives, the target audience, the budget available and how it is likely to be spent, the next decision is the content of the message. The message might be a combination of words, symbols, characters, colours, sounds, etc. At the heart of good promotional campaigns is excellent copywriting.

Copywriting

Copywriting is the act of writing selling messages. It involves both written and spoken words. The basic requirements of copywriting are as follows:

- It must sell, even if it only makes people aware and become interested in the product, it must move the customers towards a sale.
- Most people do not usually want to read advertisements. The message therefore must not waste words, it must get the message across quickly.
- If words used in a message are not well known or understood, attention is lost. Every word must be easily understood.
- Short words, short sentences, make the message quick and easy to read.

- Remember to use action verbs when trying to create a sense of urgency in getting your customer to do something. For example:

Buy	Phone	Look	Remember
Try	Send	Take	Decide
Ask	Taste	Discover	Replace

or use emotive words to create interest in altering your customers' attitudes such as:

Economical	Mouth watering	Time saving
Value for money	Satisfying	Inexpensive

Copy creates the theme for an advertising campaign and the visualiser/art director will develop ideas from the basic copy. Straplines are developed which are associated with company names or brand names to help create an image or make a statement, for example:

Never knowingly undersold
Everything we do is driven by you
Get Away
All the fun in the world
The real thing

Task 2.23

1 Can you identify which organizations the straplines above belong to: Lunn Poly; John Lewis Partnership; Ford Motor Co.; Alton Towers; Coca Cola?
2 What type of image do these straplines convey of the organization or brand?

Element 2.2, PC3

Design and layout

Copywriters are asked to think visually in trying to see how the words should be seen as well as read. Visualizers or artists and copywriters need therefore to work together when preparing an advertisement/press release or even a sales promotion.

The design of a press advertisement for example would go through a number of stages. Rough scribbles or visuals would be sketched in pencil at first until the team finally agree on two or three alternatives, or the final one. The scribbles would then be taken a stage further and would be worked up in the form of a layout (or scamp). The layout is designed to demonstrate to the agency's client, their ideas for getting the message across.

As a provisional layout there would be no artwork, photography or typesetting. This would only be provided once the campaign plans and ideas had been accepted by the client and the decision to proceed agreed. Once agreed, the layout can be worked up to its final artwork, including any photography ready for printing.

For TV or radio commercials a series of words are produced on tape, often using one of the creative teams own voiceovers. For TV commercials, a set of drawings set in TV screen

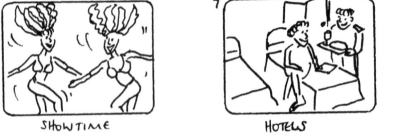

Figure 2.19 Storyboard for a ficticious commercial for Blackpool as a holiday resort

shapes or rectangles will be provided which, with the copy, tells the story of the proposed commercial. This is known as the storyboard, see Figure 2.19.

With all creative design and copy a general rule which should always be observed is KISS: keep it short – keep it simple. Never try to promote more than one or two key messages at the same time. Promoting too many messages confuses people and dilutes the effectiveness of the main message.

Implementing the campaign

When carrying out a promotional campaign we have to recognize that some promotional techniques are more effective than others in getting certain messages across to different audiences. Most of us will recognize the superiority of personal selling as a persuasive technique, particularly if we are only dealing with a small number of customers (e.g. sports wear manufacturers selling to retail shops), or where the consumer needs to be reassured that their money will be well spent (e.g. travel agent personnel advising the public as to what holidays are available and, moreover, what the destinations are like).

However, if our target market is large and spread across the whole country, then producing brochures, advertising on TV, etc. may be the most appropriate medium for delivering the message.

Selecting the media

Selecting the most appropriate media to carry our message and so meet the organization's objectives within the budget allocated is normally the job of the media buyer. When selecting the media the buyer must take into account:

● The creative characteristics of the media
● The target audience of the media.

The characteristics of various media will often lend themselves more readily to delivering certain types of message then others. Where movement and sound are considered necessary elements of the message, then TV and radio (or the production of videos, etc.) may be the most appropriate media. However, most messages are delivered very effectively by using printed materials, such as leaflets, posters, brochures, advertisements in newspapers or magazines or direct mail. These types of media offer messages in a tangible form which can provide opportunities to deliver lots of information over longer periods of time.

Choosing the right medium for the promotional message leads us to consider the questions of frequency and coverage of our target market. Coverage refers to the total number of the target market that can be covered by the medium and frequency refers to the numbers of times the message is repeated. Most media organizations will provide information about demographic distribution, size and nature of companies, spending patterns, leisure activities, and incomes of their viewers, to help you decide which medium is most appropriate.

However, coverage and frequency of media choice may also be linked to financial constraints so the organization must distinguish between media which are affordable and those that are not. Media choice must be made on the basis of cost effectiveness. Cost effectiveness of an advertisement is not simply based on good coverage, but on the frequency needed to produce the required impact on the targeted audience. No matter how well the message is presented, its effectiveness increases with repetition. However, to repeat the message time and again costs. The effectiveness of an advertisement will therefore relate to its budget – or the number of times the target market is exposed to its message or have the opportunity to see it (OTS).

Task 2.24

Working on your own, or in small groups, decide what type of media you would recommend (assuming sufficient money is available in each case) for promoting the following products and services:

- *A major theme park situated in the Midlands*
- *An exclusive keep-fit club in the centre of town*
- *New football strip for a football league club*
- *Off-peak coach tours for pensioners*
- *Heritage centre*
- *New designer trainers by Reebok*
- *New out-of-town leisure/retail complex.*

Give reasons in support of your recommendations.
Element 2.2, PC4

Scheduling the media

Having rescheduled the media and worked out all the costs, the campaign planner, together with the media buyer will draw up a media schedule. This is a plan or diary of the proposed number of advertisements (called insertions) into the press, or appearances on TV or radio, etc., over the period of the promotional campaign. The schedule will list on one side the media proposed, the number of insertions and the cost per insertion. On the other side when the insertions will take place and the total costs for the promotional campaign, together with any comments.

An example of a media schedule is provided in Table 2.3.

The schedule will be included in the final presentation made to the client on the promotional campaign. Once the media schedule has been approved, or amended, it becomes the media buyer's task to make the bookings and buy the space.

Printing materials

Whether placing advertisements in newspapers, magazines, trade press or periodicals, or whether you are producing leaflets, brochures, posters or point of sale, etc. printed materials will inevitably be required as part of your promotional campaign. The printed media allow for accurate targeting of your customers. Customer segments can be identified by analysing readership profiles of newspapers or magazines, etc. which are provided by the media organizations. Short or long messages can be sent to your market which can be read repeatedly.

In addition to advertising, leisure and tourism organizations often produce leaflets and brochures to display at their customer premises or for mailing direct to their target markets. With modern print technology and desk top publishing facilities many smaller organizations find it very acceptable to produce their own printed materials, particularly if it is for local consumption. However, where large quantities of materials are required for much larger, possibly national audiences, and where the brochure design is complicated and printed in full colour, then a professional printer is almost certainly required. Most advertising agencies will advise on choice of printer to handle work, but it is not uncommon for leisure and tourism organizations to deal with the printer direct.

No matter how large or small the printing job, when dealing with printers you should be aware of a number of things to ensure your organization's budget is used effectively.

1 As with advertising agencies, ask to see samples of their previous work and, if possible, go and see their premises. A lot can be learned from seeing how they work and what types of jobs they print.
2 Develop contacts with several printers, and always ask several printers to quote before deciding who gets the job. Competition always keeps the price keen and also tells you what you can afford.

Table 2.3 Media schedule

Media plan	Size/ length of ad	No of inserts	Cost per insert	Jan	Feb	Mar	Apr	May	June	Jul	Aug	Sep	Oct	Nov	Dec	Sub total cost	Comments
Television ITV (area?) Channel 4	Commercial																
Local radio	30 second spot																
National press	Full page; 1/2; 1/4																
Local press	Full page; 1/2; 1/4																
Free trade press	Full page; 1/2; 1/4																
Direct mailing	Packages delivered to select addresses																
Outdoor posters, bus shelters																	
Hoardings																	
Display posters																	
Promotional offers																	

3 Deciding the number of pages is important in all leaflet and brochure design. Multiples of 4 pages are inevitable for a folded sheet printed on both sides producing 4 pages. If you can design your leaflets or brochures that use 4, 8, 16 or more pages then substantial print savings can be made by printers utilizing the maximum amount of space on a sheet or roll of paper.

4 When the job is underway you must ask the printer to provide proofs of the printed job. Proofs are impressions (often in colour) taken from the film of the artwork to show how the finished job should look.

5 Always keep old artwork and copies of film used by the printers in case they can be used again in the future. It can save money on future print jobs.

Paper sizes

Brochures, sales letters, leaflets etc. should, in the interest of economy, be designed from standard paper sizes. The most common finished sizes are based upon a square metre of paper arranged in such a way so that when paper is cut and folded in half, the two sides remain the same size. For example, take one page of an A4 sheet and fold it in half, this gives you 4 sides of A5. Fold the A5 sheet in half and you get 8 sides of A6. Try it for yourself.

Paper sizes are based on what is called the 'A' series paper sizes as shown in Figure 2.20.

Direct marketing

Much of the printed material is provided for the organization's salesforce and for display at the customers' premises, for example tour operators brochures on display at a travel agents. However, many leisure and tourism organizations, today, design printed material for distributing to their target markets direct. The two main methods of distributing printed material other than by the salesforce are:

1 Door to door distribution
2 Direct mail.

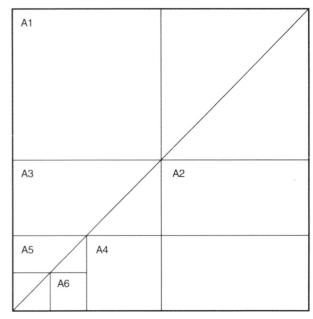

Size	Millimeters	Approximate inches
A0	841 x 1189	$33^1/_8$ x $46^3/_4$
A1	594 x 841	$22^3/_8$ x $33^1/_8$
A2	420 x 594	$16^1/_8$ x $22^3/_8$
A3	297 x 420	$11^3/_4$ x $16^1/_8$
A4	210 x 297	$8^1/_4$ x $11^3/_4$
A5	148 x 210	$5^7/_8$ x $8^1/_4$
A6	105 x 148	$4^1/_8$ x $5^7/_8$

Figure 2.20 'A' series paper sizes

Door to door distribution – This method of distribution is to do with dropping printed material through people's letterboxes. It is much less expensive than direct mail in that it doesn't seek to target particular customer groups, rather it focuses on covering all households within a given area. This can be done on a national basis (a method favoured by the football pools companies) or it can be done locally. Local restaurants, sports centres, theatres, clubs etc. often find this to be a very effective way of covering households within a given distance of their premises, or in selecting those areas or communities which it is believed will most likely respond to their message.

Direct mail – Direct mail has been around for quite some time now with companies like Readers Digest using printed letters which look like they have been typed just for you. The great advantage of direct mail is that:

- Messages can be personalized and even graphics added such as a map showing the location of the nearest retailer stocking the item to the customer's home.
- Customers who have an interest in your product can be more accurately targeted, thus increasing the effectiveness of the campaign in terms of customer response and lower costs.

The 80/20 rule (Pareto effect) where 80 per cent of an organization's sales comes from 20 per cent of its customers is of particular relevance here. Find the 20 per cent from your existing records and, by using mail merge on your computer, personalized messages can be sent to those market groups or customers who are most likely to respond.

Task 2.25

In groups decide the best ways to create an address list database for your school or college to use for mailing:

- *Details of your leisure courses.*
- *Details to parents in your area with older children in school Year 11 about a college open evening with an invitation to see the facilities and courses on offer.*

Remember, when developing a direct mail package it is important to consider the following:

- *Who is the promotion aimed at and how to persuade the public to become customers.*
- *The written message should be kept short and to the point.*
- *The emphasis should be on arousing curiosity or excitement (e.g. mark the front of the envelope 'Private' or 'Strictly Confidential').*
- *Make it easy for your target audience to reply to your message. Include a reply paid envelope, cards or coupons.*
- *Offer some inducement to reply, a mystery gift, free entry into a prize draw.*

- *Use action words such as 'Introducing new or improved', 'offer closes', 'exclusive, offer available for limited period'.*
- *Make the message appealing to your target audience by stressing the benefits of what your product can do for them.*
Element 2.2, PC4

Once the mail package is complete you now need to consider the mailing factors such as:

- *Postage costs* – discount can be obtained from the Post Office on mailings over a certain quantity
- *Reply envelope* – these can be pre-paid or simply pre-addressed back to the leisure organization.
- *Envelopes* – there are a whole range of envelope sizes designed to accommodate the standard 'A' series paper sizes. Generally the prefix 'C' is added to the paper size e.g. C4 for paper size A4 or C5 for A5 paper. Examples are given in Figure 2.21.

Task 2.26

In groups design a direct mail campaign to the industry in your local area, alerting them to the new language laboratories, training and conference facilities just built by your college. Your aim is to gain interest in the facilities and persuade them to come and visit.

- *Draft a sales letter.*
- *Decide what other promotional materials should be included in the mail package.*
- *Create the main copy lines to your promotional message which should instil interest and provide the benefits (i.e. reasons) as to why they should come and visit.*
- *Prepare some draft visuals to support your copy and show what your promotional material would look like.*
Element 2.3, PC1

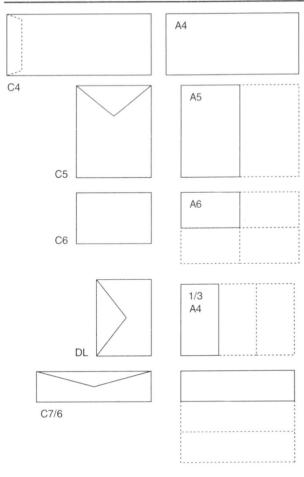

Size	Millimeters	Approximate inches
C0	917 x 1297	$36^1/_8$ x 51
C1	648 x 917	$25^1/_8$ x $36^1/_8$
C2	458 x 648	18 x $25^1/_8$
C3	324 x 458	$12^3/_4$ x 18
C4	229 x 324	9 x $12^3/_4$
C5	162 x 229	$6^3/_8$ x 9
C6	114 x 162	$4^1/_8$ x $6^3/_8$
C7	81 x 114	$3^1/_4$ x $4^1/_8$
C8	57 x 81	$2^1/_4$ x $3^1/_4$
DL	110 x 220	$4^3/_4$ x $8^5/_8$
C7/6	81 x 162	$3^1/_4$ x $6^3/_8$

Figure 2.21 'C' series envelope sizes

Evaluating the effectiveness of a campaign

In 1920 Daniel Starch suggested that for an advertisement to be effective, it must be read, believed, remembered and acted upon. With fewer forms of promotion available back in the 1920s it was probably relatively easier to measure the effectiveness of a single promotional technique such as advertising. Today, with a larger assortment of techniques available it is most unlikely that a leisure and tourism organization would use just one promotional technique, rather they would use several in combination. Evaluating the effectiveness of a whole range of promotional techniques becomes a much more difficult task – so why try?

Asked whether the large sum of money spent on promotions was worth it, the chairman of a major holiday company was reported as saying: 'I know 50 per cent of my advertising is working successfully. The problem is I don't know which 50 per cent.'

While most leisure and tourism organizations are quite happy with the effectiveness of their overall promotional campaigns, it is possible that not all the promotional techniques used are performing well and some could be wasting money. Two of the most common reasons given for evaluating campaigns are:

1 To show that money has been well spent and not wasted.
2 To show that the promotional campaign has contributed to sales.

Pre- and post testing of the market

The most common method of evaluating the success of a campaign is to test the views of a representative sample of your target market both before and after the campaign. Pre-testing will determine what proportion of the market are already aware of the organization's product and their perceptions of the product or the organization before the campaign begins. Post-testing will involve asking the same questions to another sample of the market so as to gauge what movement in awareness, attitudes or possibly sales has been achieved by the campaign.

Figure 2.22 The persuasion pendulum

All campaign objectives are basically concerned with some form of movement in persuading the target market to behave in some way. By comparing the post test results to the objectives of the campaign it will determine whether the campaign was effective or not. The persuasion pendulum in Figure 2.22 reflects the likely impact of the key promotional techniques in getting the market to move towards action over time.

Measuring the effectiveness of the promotional techniques

- The effectiveness of press or magazine advertising can be relatively easy to measure provided the advertisement includes a pre-coded response coupon. The code on the coupon identifies the magazine or newspaper from which an enquiry was received. Have a look at advertisements which carry coupons and it is likely you will see a code in the corner of the coupon such as SM25/5–1. The code often identifies the paper and the date of the insertion of the advertisement. In this case, *Sunday Mirror*, 25 May, first insertion.
- Television and radio advertising are more difficult to measure unless they are seeking a response by getting viewers to call a certain telephone number or write to a given address. This form of media advertising is often used to create or improve the

perception and image for a leisure product or service. Organizations will judge the effectiveness of their advertising over time by monitoring the effect on ultimate sales, but in the interim, pre- and post-testing of the market will provide a measure of the success or failure of their promotional advertising techniques in improving awareness or altering the behaviour of their markets in some way.

- Public relations, like television and radio, is also hard to measure because it too is often involved with building awareness and improving the image of the organization and its products. Again, pre- and post-testing is an effective measure. However, organizations can measure the amount of free editorial coverage obtained in the press or on TV etc. The number of articles, features, pictures of its products covered in the 'press' can be measured in what is called 'column inches' or those carried on TV or radio can be measured by the amount of 'air time' obtained. The value of the free coverage can be calculated against the advertising rates the media would normally charge which can then be compared to the costs incurred in putting the PR package together.
- Display again is very much involved with gaining attention and building on the perceptions and image of the product or organization and so can only effectively be measured over time using pre- and post-testing techniques. Interestingly, because of the cost of display some of the larger retails stores try and isolate this promotional technique in order to measure customer reaction. How they do this is by inviting local customers to view and make comment on changes in design of their stores. The sales of the store are then monitored over an agreed time span and compared with previously obtained sales.
- Sales promotion requires a quick response from our market, for example, to take up an offer of a free gift. The emphasis is on action which generally makes it easier for the leisure and tourism organizations to monitor its effectiveness.

- Direct marketing including selling and direct mail are relatively easier to measure because of the targeted nature of the promotional techniques. Mailings to households can include coded coupons or tickets similar to the advertisements so that responses can be accurately recorded. Selling on the other hand can be monitored against set budgets or targets to see how each salesperson is performing.

Coverage

- Element 2.2 and 2.3
- Performance criteria 1 to 4
- Core skills
  Application of numbers
  Communication
  Information technology

▪ Assignment 2.3 ▪

In teams of between five and six members you are to plan, prepare, design and evaluate a promotional campaign for your school or college. Each member of the team will represent different staff of competing advertising agencies; Gotit, Adcon, Foolum and Botchit.

Client brief

The senior management team of your school/college are about to brief the advertising agencies on taking over the college's advertising and publicity from next year. The college is concerned to improve its image within the local community and to increase its intake of students by way of more creative and effective communications with its target market.

The team are dissatisfied with its present prospectus and course literature, particularly for leisure and tourism. There would appear to be a great demand for subjects offering this type of vocational course and they would like to increase student intake numbers, but the competition is hotting up. They wish to heavily promote one particular leisure or tourism course and so assess the effectiveness of a promotional campaign in achieving the above objectives.

Task 1

Form teams of four or five members and decide roles based on each other's skills, experience and resources. This will help the group in carrying out the tasks below.

Task 2

Agency groups to research the college's current prospectus and advertising literature on leisure and tourism courses and to determine the likely target markets for the courses and the negative and positive aspects of the past advertising campaigns in attracting the target markets.

Task 3

Agency to determine what further information is required from the college and to agree a series of questions to be asked at the briefing session.

Task 4

Attend briefing session and confirm with the college the objectives of the campaign, its target audience, the resources and budget available, etc.

Task 6

Conduct the presentation in the fourth week, in which all members must take part. The presentation should take approximately 15 minutes and must include visual examples of how the message is to be creatively put across.

Task 5

Prepare ideas for putting across a promotional message which are to be presented to the college's senior management team in four week's time. The campaign proposals should include:

- Outline of the college's objectives
- Statement of target market(s)
- Message content (copylines, straplines, etc.)
- Choice of media (including frequency and coverage)
- Schedule of timings
- Visuals of ads

Task 7

All agencies to review their campaign proposals in light of the college management decision as to who won the advertising account. The groups to write a report outlining how their campaign met with or fell short of the college's objectives, target markets and resources. The report should make recommendations for improvements to similar future campaigns.

LOOKING AFTER CUSTOMERS

Effective customer service

In this section we aim to:

- Find out who our customers are
- Look at the importance of customer care
- Establish what customers want from staff
- Explore customer satisfaction
- Investigate different customer care policies that companies use
- Examine the ways in which we can improve our customer care skills.

We are all customers in different situations and we know how we would like to be treated by staff. This section tries to establish good and bad practices and help you to make the most of opportunities to promote the products and services of the leisure or tourism facility.

Figure 3.1

The customer

Who or what are customers?

The Oxford English Dictionary gives two definitions:

1 A person who buys goods or services from a shop or business.
2 A person one has to deal with.

Leisure and tourism facilities need customers, that is obvious, and these are called by various titles – guests, visitors, clients, users, the public, punters, tourists, other staff. According to this, we are all customers at different times.

Task 3.1

Think of some different situations when you have been a customer. Was the experience good, or could it have been improved?
Element 3.1, PC1

We all have different ideas about how we should be treated and these expectations, as they are called, are very important. How one person is treated is not necessarily acceptable to another and judging how to deal with customers is an important skill.

People have different motivations (the reason for doing something) and the reasons for buying different goods and services vary with the individual.

For example, my reasons for joining a swimming club may be very different from yours. I may have expectations such as keeping fit and remaining healthy. I may also want to meet different people. Your reasons may be that you are good at swimming and you want to take part in competitions or you may join because your friends have joined.

What is communication?

There are many answers, but people usually say that people talk to one another, or they write messages.

So if I communicated 'Nadolig Llawen', perhaps only a few people who speak Welsh would understand.

This is one of the most important aspects of communication, that we understand the message someone is trying to pass on.

By the way, I wished you 'Merry Christmas'.

Task 3.2

Think of other examples of communication apart from speaking.
Element 3.1, PC4

Customers also make decisions about products and services and staff. They expect the product to reach certain standards, and if this does not happen they are dissatisfied and possibly will not use the company again.

Task 3.3

Think of a situation when you were trying to buy something or you were asking for information and the process went wrong.

● *What was the situation and what were you trying to achieve?*
● *Why did it go wrong?*
● *Was it your fault or that of someone else?*
● *How could it have been corrected?*
Element 3.1, PC4

The important part of this exercise is how the situation could have been corrected.

As well as the product or service being important to the customer, as people they want to be treated well and to be taken seriously.

Task 3.4

In pairs, work through the following situation, one person being the customer, the other being the receptionist. You have to solve the problem somehow:

You have been working out at the gym/aerobics exercise class and when you return to the changing room your outdoor clothes are wet. This is probably because they have been cleaning the changing room. Obviously you are angry, and more so because it is lunchtime and you have to return to work. You go to see the receptionist and . . .
Element 3.1, PC2, 3, 4 and 5

The importance of customer care

As we have already mentioned, leisure and tourism facilities need customers in order to survive.

Customers want to be happy and satisfied with the service – they do not want an unpleasant experience. They also want to be liked and cared for.

Satisfied customers tend to return to the business. Dissatisfied customers will take their custom elsewhere. With a wide choice of leisure facilities today in most towns and cities, customers can take their business to the next pool, park, sports centre or cinema.

> Good news travels fast,
> Bad news travels even faster!

Satisfied customers are likely to tell their friends and encourage them to use the venue. Word of mouth is the best form of advertising – and the cheapest!

Dissatisfied customers will not return and they will again tell their friends of bad experiences so that they will also influence potential new customers.

Good customer relations, particularly in the service or hospitality industry, can turn first-time 'buyers' into regular customers. Skills and attitudes in good customer relations or customer care are vital for the business to succeed.

Figure 3.2

Task 3.5

What areas do you think are important to include in a customer care policy?
Element 3.1, PC1, 2 and 3

Customer care does not simply mean being pleasant with customers. It also means working towards the goals of the organization as well as meeting the needs of the customer and making it easy for the customer to return and bring a friend.

In leisure and tourism, as in other service industries, (those industries that serve the public) competition is increasing and customers are setting high standards. Good customer service is now more important to business success than ever.

Good customer care policies mean making the customer feel important and showing them that their custom is valued and that we really do want their business.

Task 3.6

If we want to give a good service to customers, we need to find out what their needs, wants and wishes are.

How would you go about this?
Element 3.1, PC4

Hopefully your list includes some or all of the following items:

- Observe
- Listen
- Ask
- Monitor

Task 3.7

How would staff such as receptionists, doormen, catering staff, bar staff, and duty managers help in the observation and listening sections?

The people mentioned above can watch, listen and be receptive to clues given by customers, such as signs of happiness or signs of displeasure.

Some customers will talk a lot, but most need encouragement. Traditionally, places of relaxation such as saunas, health clinics, hairdressers and bars – where listening is part of the service – can be useful sources of information.

Some staff are happier than others at talking to people and putting them at their ease.

Many companies are afraid to ask their customers what they want, although this is gradually changing. Generally, people are very happy to tell you!

Task 3.8

With a partner, discuss your expectations of the following – then swap round: a bank, a fitness centre, a cinema, a disco, a restaurant.
Element 3.1, PC5

Have you ever been asked for your comments on facilities and services?

Did you complete the form? If not, why not?

There are many less formal ways of obtaining information, such as:

- Casual conversation
- Suggestion boxes
- Surveys
  - face to face
  - short questionnaires
- Feedback to duty manager by forms, complaints and thank-yous.

Task 3.9

What sort of things would you expect from a leisure facility? Think of one in your area to help you.

Does your list include any of the following?

- No queuing
- Car parking space
- Telephone bookings of tickets and courts
- Credit card transactions
- Pleasant atmosphere
- Trouble-free environment
- Top-class instruction
- A warm, friendly atmosphere
- Competitive prices and value for money
- Fast attention to requirements
- Cleanliness in all areas, including toilets
- Politeness and pleasantness from staff
- Good security measures.

Task 3.10

Have you ever made a telephone booking? What happens?
Element 3.1, PC4

Customer expectations and satisfaction

Staff have to put themselves into the customer's shoes.

Task 3.11

What do your feel like when you:

- *Stand in a queue*
- *Are kept waiting*
- *Receive no smile or recognition*
- *Receive no apology*
- *Are ignored by staff who are more interested in talking to each other*
- *Are made to look small.*

Element 3.2, PC4

I expect that the answers are not very positive. The impression you have been given is unpleasant.

Recognizing this, then, should encourage us to treat our customers in the way that we would like to be treated.

We need to remember that we are dependent on customers, not they who are dependent on us.

Task 3.12

How should you react to customers? Make a list of the things you should do.
Element 3.1, PC1, 3 and 4

Does your list match mine?

- Look at the customer – eye contact establishes warmth and trust.
- Call the customer by name if possible.
- Smile, say 'hello' and sound friendly.
- Give the customer your full attention.
- Be polite – customers will probably be polite in return.
- Offer to help – this can allow us to find out the problem quickly and sort it out quickly.

Task 3.13

What should you expect from an after-sales service?

As the name implies, this part of service takes place after the customer has made a purchase. Generally, even where membership systems and registrations provide lists of known interested people, there is very little follow-up or promotional work carried out.

Task 3.14

Find some sort of membership scenario in a leisure and tourism facility, e.g. sports centre, theatre or cinema.

What sort of follow-up or after-sales service do they operate? For example, do they send out information on promotions?

Element 3.1, PC1 and 5

Once we have identified our customers, we should communicate with them regularly to show them they are valued and that they have not been forgotten.

Above all, we should try to provide a flexible customer care policy.

Traditionally there may have been situations where the customer had to take it or leave it. Leisure and tourism is now more diverse – meaning that staff have to be more flexible as greater choice is given.

Obviously this shows that a flexible approach is the best one. However, staff do still need to follow the basic guidelines of the company and seek help if there is a problem.

Task 3.15

Having read the last section, put together a list of points that need consideration when designing a customer care scheme.
Element 3.1, PC1, 2, 3 and 4

Your list should include the following points:

1 Human relations skills – developing these skills requires knowledge of the customers, the facility or organization and about your roles and responsibilities to the organization and the customer.
2 Service skills – a product will remain basically the same no matter who the customer is. A service provides a meeting point between the facility and the customer where things can go right, but also where things can go wrong.
3 Customer satisfaction – satisfied customers will return and possibly bring their friends. However, poor customer service will place

the facility at a disadvantage. People should be treated with attention, consideration and understanding.

4 Points of contact. Within many aspects of leisure the customer will come into contact with staff – reception, during their activity, catering, etc. Every point of contact is an opportunity to give a good impression and demonstrate the customer care policy.

5 Customers know what they want – so ask them.

6 Get it right first time – if you make a promise to contact someone, then do so.

7 Complaints are not necessarily bad – they can present new opportunities. Listen, apologize, question, sympathize and agree on a course of action. Then make sure you follow it up.

8 Good customer care helps prevent problems.

Task 3.16

Think of the staff at a local swimming pool or leisure complex. What is your impression of them? What do you remember about them?
Element 3.1, PC5

9 Staff attitude and appearance. First impressions count. If you smile, it is likely that people will smile back. Impressions keep some customers and lose others. The way the staff look and behave will have an important effect on customers.

10 Make sure that if you promise to do something for a customer, then you carry it out.

11 Provide an after-sales service.

12 Train staff in the company's policy on customer care.

Customer care skills

We have discussed the advantages of a good customer care policy and now we need to review the actual skills that we can use.

We are going to discuss information under the following headings:

- Non-verbal communication (NVC)
- Face-to-face communication
- Telephone techniques
- Communication in writing.

Non-verbal communication

Task 3.17

Do you ever 'people watch'? Do you notice how they react to each other – you can find out quite a lot of information without even hearing what people are saying to each other.

Think of two people having an argument. Write down their body movements, their expressions. How would you know they were angry without even listening to what they were saying?
Element 3.1, PC4

Unfortunately, each of us makes judgements about others. For example, you probably automatically nod in approval when you meet someone who looks, talks and thinks like you. Your face, body language and words may automatically show that you approve of the other person.

On the other hand, some characteristics we notice in others may put us off. If someone dresses very smartly, has short hair and is clean-shaven, they may not approve of beards or long hair.

We tick off a list of things that are not 'right' about other people. The reaction does not just

Figure 3.3

go on inside our heads – our faces, body language and words could show how we feel.

When others live up to our expectations, we feel comfortable with them; but when they do not, we are uneasy and perhaps even feel threatened.

We cannot consciously change our opinions overnight, but we can be aware of our reactions and attempt to control them.

Face-to-face communication

Task 3.18

When you are helping someone with a query, what should you do? How should you act?
Element 3.1, PC4

Does your list agree with mine?

● **Courtesy**   Effective communication is always polite and should avoid:

- Interrupting
- Contradicting
- 'Showing off' to impress others
- Making someone 'look small'.

Task 3.19

These are just a few of the things to avoid. Can you think of any more?

● **Listening**   Failing to listen to someone is not only rude, but can lead to mistakes, so pay attention to the speaker and show that you are following.

- **Style**   Choose the correct manner for the situation. Do not use jargon and choose your words and expressions carefully. It is easy to give offence but difficult to overcome its effect.
- **Mannerisms**   Avoid irritating or discourteous mannerisms of speech, gesture or posture. Do not fiddle with pencils or doodle.
- **Thinking**   Think before you speak. Show that you can see more than one point of view.
- **Timing**   Choose the right moment to speak. Sometimes it is better to let others have their say first.

Did you realize how complicated it can be to talk to people? This brings us to the use of the telephone.

Telephone techniques

Task 3.20

Make a list of guidelines for using the telephone.
Element 3.1, PC4

1 Always use a suitable greeting. Many companies use standard phrases such as 'Hello – Debbie speaking, how can I help you?' This has two effects. The first is to let the caller know they have the right number and the second is to allow the caller to tune in to the voice, accent, etc. of the person answering.
2 Remember the caller cannot see your face for reactions, so sound decisive, concerned, interested and confident and remember to smile, as this can be picked up over the telephone.

3 Make notes of names, addresses and phone numbers and other key information.
4 No matter how difficult, try to remain calm and do not lose your temper.
5 Remember to close the call politely.

Task 3.21

With a partner, choose one of the following situations as an exercise in telephone technique:

1 A customer wants to reserve a squash court – make the booking.
2 A customer rings with a complaint about a badminton court being double booked.
3 A customer rings with an enquiry about the availability of concert tickets. Help them make the booking.

Discuss the results with the rest of your group and decide where improvements could be made.
Element 3.1, PC4 and 5

Communication in writing

Usually we would communicate with customers through letters. Standard letter formats can be found in the Resource Pack to accompany this book. However, the following list of points will help in preparing any written message:

1 Decide what the aim of the message is, and keep that firmly in mind.
2 Plan the points before starting to write.
3 Make sure the ideas are clearly laid out.
4 Make sure the information is relevant.
5 Keep it simple.
6 Make sure it is logical and one idea moves on to the next.
7 Remember who is going to receive the letter.
8 Write a clear action requirement or request.
9 Be polite and tactful.
10 Be positive.

Policies and strategies

So, what do customers want? Customer service can be broken down into four areas:

1 **Friendly service** This is more than simply being polite. Customers want to feel that their needs are important and that they are important.

Task 3.22

How would you make the customer feel they are important?
Element 3.1, PC3

Hopefully you have included things such as listening to the customer, being interested, giving accurate information and answering customers' questions. Making the customer feel important also means giving warm and friendly responses at all times (be particularly aware of when you are feeling 'out of sorts' – do not take it out on the customer), and being reassuring, especially when customers are angry or upset.

2 **Flexibility** Being able to help the customer with their problems or circumstances and making the system work for them rather than the customer fitting into the system. Customers do not want to hear 'No'. They want you to work out a way to get them what they want or need.

3 **Resolving (sorting out) problems** There are two parts to this. Firstly, when a customer has a problem they need to know that you will help them find the answer even if you need to ask someone to help you. They do not want to explain the problem to lots of different people.

Secondly, they may also want you to help with non-business problems – such as a flat tyre in the car park. Possibly you could contact a breakdown service such as the AA/RAC.

4 **Recovery** None of us are perfect and mistakes do happen. However, customers want them to be corrected quickly and to their satisfaction. They want the mistake to be put right quickly. Hopefully these practices would make the customer loyal to your company and encourage them to use the company again.

This list of requirements is probably the basis for many companies' customer care policies.

A policy is simply a plan of action that the company or person has decided to follow. The

Figure 3.4

other term sometimes used is 'strategy', and this simply means a plan to achieve something.

Many companies do not have formal rigid rules that staff have to follow. They rely on their employees to sort situations out themselves.

Task 3.23

Which do you think is best – a set of guidelines to help staff deal with customers or leaving it to the individual staff to sort out?

Make a list of what areas should be covered by these guidelines.

In this section we have reviewed all the aspects of customer care ranging from what it is to looking at how companies within leisure and tourism operate policies. Hopefully you have also gained information on what makes a good customer care scheme and where improvements can be made. That is the theory – it is not always that easy in practise!

▪ Assignment 3.1 ▪

When people join a new company, they should undergo some kind of induction scheme. This helps the new employee to settle into the new working environment, to cover any legal requirements and to meet the people they are going to work with.

Scenario

As part of an induction scheme, customer care should play a major part because we are a people-based industry. You have been asked to put together a customer care plan so that new employees know how to deal with customers and the importance of good customer relations.

Details

1 Describe to the new employee the different types of people they may meet.
2 State why customer care is so important.
3 Suggest ideas to help the new employee deal with customers in the following situations:
   (a) face-to-face communication
   (b) communications with individuals
   (c) communications with groups
   (d) written communications, i.e. letters
   (e) telephone communications.
4 Explain why listening is so important.
5 Give examples of various situations or jobs where you would need customer care skills.

Providing information

In this section we are going to look at:

● The importance of the employee knowing about the organization
● Knowledge of local, regional and national publications as a source of information
● The needs for the ability to give clear instructions.

Knowledge of the organization

Task 3.24

Think about either your part-time job or your work placement, or your school.

Write down what you know about the organization. Is it large or small? Is it linked to another outlet? Who makes the decisions about policy? Who is in charge?

Element 3.2, PC1 and 2

You may be surprised about how much you know of the organization. This information is very important to us and also to our customers.

Task 3.25

If someone asks you a question to which you do not know the answer, what do you do?
Element 3.2, PC3

Hopefully you answered that you found the information out from someone else. Who is that person? A colleague? A superior? The cleaner? How accurate and reliable is that information likely to be?

Task 3.26

You have gone into a leisure centre asking for information about membership and facilities. The person behind reception is unable to help you and they cannot find anyone who can.

Write down how you feel and what your impression of this organization is.

How do the rest of your group feel?
Element 3.2, PC1, 2 and 3

You probably mentioned that the image given was not very good. Perhaps you mentioned you felt confused or even angry that they were unable to deal with a simple request.

We have all come across situations like this, and one of the aims of customer care is to avoid such situations arising.

Naturally we want our customers to gain a good impression of us and, as a result, our company. Therefore our knowledge of the organization, the products we offer and the industry generally all help us to give a good impression to our customers.

However, no one has all the answers. No one could be expected to be able to answer every query. Customers generally understand this.

It is important that if you are asked a question to which you do not know the answer, you explain to the customer that you are going to find out the answer and you will let them know.

It is very important that if you say you will contact someone with an answer, then you do – even if it is to keep them informed about how far the query has been taken. It is easy to create a bad impression in this situation.

Publications

There is a wealth of publicity available within leisure and tourism.

Task 3.27

Collect information about your local area. Put the information together to show the events and facilities that are available to the public.
Element 3.2, PC1, 2, 3, 4 and 5

You have collected and assessed a lot of local information in the above task to give an idea of the range of facilities that are available to the customer.

Some leisure and tourism jobs would expect you to be aware of what is available, e.g. when working in a Tourist Information Office.

In this example, people go to these venues to gain information and to ask questions of the staff. Other aspects of the industry will also rely on the specialist knowledge of staff.

Task 3.28

Where do you find out about the industry? Make a list of the different places you might find information.
Element 3.2, PC3

Perhaps your list is similar to mine:
Newspapers, brochures, maps, guides, lists and programmes of sporting events and arts venues, magazines.

All of these produce large amounts of information which is intended either to encourage the customer to attend or to give information about the latest developments within the industry.

At times, it is very difficult to gain all the information you may need. However, with experience you are likely to know the general questions people ask and each query you deal with will teach you something.

Giving directions

Task 3.29

Working in pairs, explain to your partner how to get from where you are at present to:

- *The bus station*
- *The nearest newsagent*
- *The nearest swimming pool*
- *The nearest cinema.*

Do not assume that everyone has transport – try explaining using bus, train or by walking (within reason).
Element 3.2, PC4 and 5

How did you find this task? Was it easy or difficult? Giving accurate directions of either how to find a certain venue or giving instructions on how to complete forms is not necessarily easy.

In the above task, did you draw a map? Did you write down the instructions? Did you rely on the person's memory? Which is likely to be the most accurate and appropriate method?

Always try to be logical when giving information. The details should follow on from one point to another, particularly when giving instructions and following a certain procedure.

▪ Assignment 3.2 ▪

Scenario

People are individuals and customers vary greatly. They have very different needs and expectations.

This assignment is designed to help us to provide customer service to people as individuals.

Details

1 Explain why it is important to the customer that employees have an accurate knowledge about the organization and how it works.
2 Which magazines and other publications are available to help employees gain information about leisure and tourism. Give a short description of each.
3 Research a leisure/tourism provider in your local area.
4 Describe the range of customers that they have and the sort of provision the company gives.
5 How does the company provide for customers with special requirements? Are they able to give good customer service to:
   (a) wheelchair clients
   (b) hard of hearing clients
   (c) non-English speaking visitors
   (d) people of different ages
   (e) business visitors?

Selling and customer care

In this section we are going to be reviewing the following areas:

- Selling and the importance of sales to leisure organizations
- The importance of records
- Different types of records and recording methods
- Data storage.

Selling skills

There are many different ways in which to sell a product.

Task 3.30

Make a list of the ways in which we can sell leisure and tourism. How do we gain people's interest?
Element 3.3, PC2

Figure 3.5

There are many tools available and I am sure your list includes advertising in the press, on radio and television, through guides, word of mouth and public relations.

Public relations involves communicating a good image of the establishment to the customer and community and it can involve things like charity contributions, litter control near premises (such as McDonald's) or reductions for certain categories such as the unwaged or senior citizens. This may attract press attention, so giving free advertising.

Other activities may include ideas such as presentations at the launch of a new product where an image is sold to the customer.

Even when we already have an established clientele, customer care skills are very important.

The customer may already be using a venue but may not realize the range of services offered. By talking to customers and finding out about them, it may then be easy to introduce other aspects of the product to them.

Why do we need to pay so much attention to sales and selling? The main answer is that this will hopefully lead to customer satisfaction.

If customers are satisfied with the level of service they are given, then this is likely to lead to them returning to the venue, so providing repeat business.

As a result of repeat business, the facility will create more income from customers and remain in business, which will hopefully expand, creating more jobs, more security and so on.

The importance of records

Records are very important to any company or organization, no matter whether it is in the public or private sector of ownership. Records are also a legal requirement, particularly for Inland Revenue and VAT purposes. If accurate, up-to-date paperwork is not kept, prosecution through the legal system can result.

Different companies will have their own standard records, but the following information will give an idea of what is required.

Task 3.31

You are the manager of a leisure complex that offers refreshments. On a Tuesday morning you have a Mother and Toddlers swimming session.

Think of some other facilities that you might introduce to this group for their families. Make a list.
Element 3.3, PC1 and 2

Task 3.32

Why do you think it is important to keep records? How many reasons can you think of that are different from ours?
Element 3.3, PC3

Perhaps in this task you mentioned the swimming club that runs through the school holidays for older children, or the fact that a water aerobics class is held during the week for senior citizens.

There are lots of different types of records that are kept in various leisure organizations. Make a list of those you can think of and where they would be used.

Records and recording methods

We are going to look at records under two different headings:

- Records of money transactions
- Customer records.

Money transactions

Where cash is paid by customers for a service within a leisure facility, as well as being charged to either the customer or the customer's account, there must be some form of book-keeping (a way of keeping financial records) to record these transactions.

Obviously the system and how complex it is will vary according to the size of the organization and the amount of business that it has.

Figure 3.6

under the appropriate headings, e.g. sports hall hire, swimming pool admissions. Table 3.1 shows an example.

All the columns should be added vertically (down) and horizontally (across) and the totals should agree. This is called a 'cross balance'.

Task 3.33

Think of a leisure complex or centre near you.

What sort of facilities does it provide for its customers? Make a list. How popular is it?

List all the records of the different transactions you think the facility will need to keep records of and to which part of the leisure complex it will relate – e.g. swimming pool, sports hall.
Element 3.3, PC3 and 4
Element 3.4, PC4

Task 3.34

Using the example given in Table 3.1, carry out a cross balance. Summarize the totals for each section and give the overall daily sales figure.
Element 3.4, PC2 and 4

From this exercise we can see that some sort of summary needs to be kept to give easily understood records. This may have many names, but it may simply be known as a summary book! It is used to record a breakdown of the total sales and their relevant methods of payment.

This information placed on the summary sheet is taken from all the sales from the facility

These figures may then be placed on to other records to give an overview of how the income of the facility is being generated. For example, daily records could be compared – it is likely that income and so usage of the facility will be greater at weekends than during the week. This information could then be used, by marketing people for example, to generate higher usage on quiet days.

Table 3.1

	Admissions	Sports hall	Swimming pool	Cinema	Restaurant	Total
General	130.00			85.00	225.00	440.00
Swimming Club			95.00			95.00
Karate Club		45.00				45.00
Eastham High School			150.00			150.00
Badminton Club		60.00				60.00
Total	**130.00**	**105.00**	**245.00**	**85.00**	**225.00**	**790.00**

This analysis could also be taken a stage further to break down the various methods of payment.

Task 3.35

Think of how you could pay for something – a product or service – other than with money.
Element 3.4, PC1 and 3

In the example we have already reviewed, it is unlikely that the school would pay with cash – they are more likely to pay by cheque or some sort of money transfer to the leisure centre.

Again, many people pay larger sums by cheque, credit or debit card, as it is convenient and saves them having to carry large amounts of money.

Task 3.36

What is a 'float'?

The float

Every facility needs a 'float' of money to allow it to give a service to customers – change for admissions, to allow catering areas and other sales points to operate. It is like an advance loan.

The amount of money needed in a permanent float will be determined by three main factors:

- The price charged in the different areas
- The number of transactions carried out
- The methods of payment used by customers. Obviously you do not give change on credit card, debit card or cheque transactions!

When dealing with transactions it is essential that the total cash, cheques, credit and debit card and petty cash vouchers (dealt with in the next sub-section) is equal to the total of the record of receipts and the float. Again a cross balance is taking place. This is a way of checking that the figures are correct.

If there are any shortages or overs, the situation should be investigated and the procedure followed for reporting them. This will vary depending on the organization.

When the person checking the money wants to make sure the money is correct, the permanent float should be subtracted from the total cash and the remainder should equal the total of the cash column in the summary record.

Petty cash book

Task 3.37

What is 'petty cash'?
Element 3.4, PC4

Most facilities keep a petty cash book to record all small items of expenditure. The safest method of keeping the records of petty cash is similar to that of a 'float'.

It means that the cashier is provided with a fixed sum of cash out of which small payments are made. This is known as the imprest system.

Normally the employee pays out money on behalf of the company, obtains a receipt and is then repaid by the cashier. The voucher is signed by both the cashier and the person claiming the money as proof that the money has been claimed.

Task 3.38

Design a petty cash voucher in order to record all the relevant information – do not forget the spaces for date and signatures.
Element 3.4, PC4

The petty cash book shows the total amount of float received and records of all amounts paid out, which are then analysed under various headings, usually related to products or services provided by that establishment.

Task 3.39

Look at the following information and then place it under the correct heading in the petty cash book. We have completed the first one for you.

Sundries			
	Stationery and books	2.40	VAT 0.49
	Cleaning materials	0.38	
Interview Mr James	Expenses	11.40	VAT 2.00
Stamps		19.00	VAT 0.00
Data post		13.26	VAT 2.32
Photocopying		6.39	VAT 1.12
Cleaning materials		1.90	VAT 0.33
Interview Mrs Smith	Expenses	8.17	VAT 1.43

Float	Date	Desc.	Total	Stationery and books	Cleaning materials	Travel expenses	Postage	VAT
200.00	10/7	Float						
	10/7	Sundrs	3.20	2.40	0.38			0.42

Element 3.4, PC4

Receipts

The cashier's main duty is to receive payments. This includes receiving payment by cash, credit and debit cards, charge cards and vouchers.

Money may also arrive from other departments such as coffee bars, vending machines and restaurants and perhaps shop facilities selling equipment and sportswear. Details of the takings will be summarized on a departmental paying-in slip.

For all money received, whether from staff or customers, a receipt is required as proof of payment – even if payment is made by cheque.

The system used will depend on the billing methods used in the organization. However, receipts normally include the name of the payer and details the amount received in words and figures, the method of payment, the date and signature of the cashier.

Task 3.40

Design a receipt issued by a leisure organization or a travel/tourism outlet when producing receipts.

Also produce a checklist for yourself or other staff to use when issuing and recording receipts.
Element 3.4, PC4

Hopefully your list looks something like this:

1 Check the amount of cash received.
2 Record in duplicate (twice) these figures on a receipt, also including:
   (i)   name of payer and details
   (ii) amount received
   (iii) method of payment
   (iv) signature and date.
3 Pass a copy to the payer.

Security

This is very important when dealing with money. Cash is a temptation to thieves and members of staff may also succumb to this temptation as easily as a stranger.

There is a duty to ensure that the customer is only asked to pay for those goods or services which they have used and that they are charged for all goods and services used.

If you are authorized to deal with payments during a shift, then you are also responsible for the security and safety of all the money in the cash drawer.

Task 3.41

Make a list of rules to follow when in charge of a payment point.

Does your list agree with mine?

- Never leave the cash point unattended.
- Never hand over or accept any form of payment (cash, cheque, vouchers or tokens) without the correct paperwork.
- Never allow anyone except the customer or an authorized person to look at anyone else's account.
- Never allow anyone without proper authorization into the payment point area.
- If adjustments to bills are necessary, get the proper authorization and signature before doing so.
- When anyone's honesty is in question or doubt, immediately contact a supervisor.

Figure 3.7

Computerized systems

Up to this point we have concentrated on manual systems of recording information. Many organizations now use computerized systems that save time and money.

There are many computer programs available and if a computerized system is used then obviously the organization will have its own procedures which must be followed.

Task 3.42

Make a list of the advantages and disadvantages of using a computer to the store the records needed by the facility. Give examples of the situations in which it can be used.

Customer records

Customer records are becoming increasingly important to the leisure facility. They record relevant information about customers that may be used for future membership and marketing purposes.

The information may be used to notify customers of forthcoming events in which they may be interested, as information about the facility's usage by people can be stored. For example, Mr Smith may have a regular booking for a squash court and so may be interested in a squash tournament featuring the sport's personalities.

Task 3.43

Can you think of any other information or application customer records may have?
Element 3.4, PC4

Incentives may also be offered to regular clients to encourage loyalty. These may include:

● Discount after a certain number of visits
● Special promotions to encourage family use of the facility

Thoughts and comments on customer satisfaction and improvements for the facility are encouraged.

The customer records can be part of a computer program, which can be easily analysed for effective marketing or a more personal service with information being recalled quickly.

Data storage

We have discussed in detail the different records that may be available to a facility and manual and computerized systems.

Obviously the storage of manually produced records requires space and time to achieve a reliable working system, whereas computer systems automatically store information for retrieval at a later date.

There are many companies that produce and sell customer information – one of the reasons we all receive 'junk mail'. As a result, legislation has been introduced which limits the amount of information that is held on computers about individuals.

Although it is not your responsibility to design the computer packages in use within your company, you need to be aware of the Data Protection Act which limits the amount and type of information you can place on computer about people.

Companies and organizations are also required to register with a bureau to inform the authorities that they will be storing information about customers on computer systems.

▪ Assignment 3.3 ▪

Scenario

Selling goods and services to customers is very important as otherwise the company may go out of business. This is particularly important in leisure and tourism facilities.

Details

1 Explain why selling is so important. Give information under the following headings:

(a) customer satisfaction
(b) repeat business
(c) financial benefits
(d) increased business.

2 Describe the different ways that customers may be encouraged to buy further goods and services. The following headings may be useful:
(a) creating a good impression
(b) starting a conversation
(c) open and closed questions
(d) overcoming objections
(e) handling complaints.

3 Why do you think it may be difficult to sell leisure and tourism products?

4 In a role-play situation, take turns to try to sell a leisure/tourism product to another member of your group. Assess how easy/difficult this was and put the results in your portfolio.

Providing customer service

In this section we aim to:

● Look at what we can do to find out what our customers want and then identify the most important need first
● Make sure we deal with customers in the most suitable manner
● Review how we communicate with our customers
● Deal with unusual or misleading queries
● Look at the health and safety legislation and our responsibilities
● Assess our dealings with customers accurately

There may be reference to some of the work we have already done in the first section, but this will be useful for revision before we build on and apply that information.

Figure 3.8

Customers' needs

We have already discussed the different names that customers are sometimes called.

Task 3.44

Recall some of the different words we used.
Element 3.1, PC1

Now we are going to look at some of the different categories our customers may fall into.

Some people will be old – perhaps hard of hearing and not very quick to answer you. This does not mean that they do not understand.

Task 3.45

How would you find out, tactfully, if a customer had hearing problems? How would you deal with this?
Element 3.4, PC1

Our society today is multicultural, which means that people have different backgrounds and possibly that English is not their first language. We also serve lots of tourists from foreign countries and their English will not necessarily be good.

If they do not understand you the first time, do not just shout at them – they probably won't be deaf – but try and explain or question again using different words, perhaps simpler ones.

Task 3.46

A tourist to this country has asked you for directions to the shopping centre and their English is not very good. Give those directions in the simplest terms you can.

Was that difficult? Would the person have arrived at their required destination?
Element 3.4, PC2, 3, 5 and 6

Task 3.47

Can you think of any other customers who may need special attention?
Element 3.4, PC1

Perhaps your list has more on it than mine, but I thought of physically disabled people and people with special dietary requirements as well as the problems posed by large groups of people using facilities.

Task 3.48

In teams, think of the building that you are working in. Does it cater for people who are in wheelchairs? Is the environment adapted for them to use it?
Element 3.4, PC1 and 2

Special dietary requirements

- **Religious**   I include two examples here. Firstly, Jewish diets. Kosher foods involve preparation in a certain way and animals must be slaughtered according to very strict rules. Pork is not eaten, as pigs are thought of as unclean.
  Secondly, Hindu diets. Hindus regard the cow as sacred and it cannot be killed for food. Orthodox (very strict) Hindus will not eat food from any animal that has been killed.
- **Health**   There are many reasons why people need to follow careful diets, but perhaps the best examples are diabetic diets where sugar intake has to be carefully monitored or low cholesterol diets where cholesterol levels have to be checked.
- **Moral**   Vegetarians object to the killing of animals for food and so live on a diet of fruit and vegetables and perhaps milk, eggs and fish.

If food is provided as part of the service in a leisure facility such as a sports centre, swimming pool, theatre or cinema, different customer requirements need to be taken into account. Sometimes our customers will have more than one requirement.

Task 3.49

If someone falls over and cuts a leg while on their way to buy an admission ticket to a swimming pool, what should you do?
Element 3.4, PC3

Hopefully you said that the cut required first aid and not that you should sell them a ticket! How did you make this decision? Probably by looking at the person.

We take in a lot of information through sight and hearing. You may have seen the customer fall, or you may have heard them scream, so you would know there may be a problem. You would probably then ask if they need help.

Therefore we use our senses to assess a situation. If you are ever unsure, ask customers in order to get the information that is going to help you to help them.

Dealing with customers

In the first section of this Unit we discussed the different ways in which we can deal with customers – in writing, over the telephone or face to face. But how do you know what to say or do?

This skill obviously develops with experience and you will know when you can joke with customers and when you should not.

However you decide to use your own 'people skills', remember that the customer and the company will have certain expectations of you.

You will be expected to be polite to the customer and not to be off-hand or rude. The tone that you use in your voice can give the other person information other than the words you use. It can show happiness, boredom, anger, frustration, lack of interest and can encourage or discourage a customer to react well or badly to the information.

So, in order to keep the problems that can be created to a minimum, we should always try to sound interested, aware, caring and as if we want to help people. After all we are in the 'people' business.

Task 3.50

What are the different ways that we can communicate with customers?

Make a list and show some of the problems that could arise with each.
Element 3.4, PC2 and 3

Whichever of the different ways we use to give information to our customers – through leaflets (written), over the telephone or face to face – we still give an impression of ourselves and our company.

Task 3.51

What sort of impression do you want to give customers about:

1 Yourself
2 The company you work for.

How can you achieve this?
Element 3.4, PC2, 3, 5 and 6

Queries

Task 3.52

What would you do if a customer asked you something you did not know the answer to?

How would you sort out the problem?
Element 3.4, PC1 and 2

When any of us start a new job this situation is going to arise quite frequently – no matter what level of qualification you have. Hopefully this will only be until you are familiar with the way

Figure 3.9

the new company works and the way in which they deal with problems.

Probably a colleague will be asked to show you systems and how to deal with queries until you have settled in.

If you are not sure what to do when you have a query, always ask. Never simply give an answer or say you 'don't know'. It is part of your responsibility to find the answer, both for the customer and yourself, in case you are asked the same thing by someone else.

If you are unable to help the customer there and then, make a note of the query and take a name and telephone number from the customer. When you have found out the answer, contact them to let them know. Do this as soon as possible after the enquiry.

If colleagues are too busy, then perhaps a supervisor would be able to assist. Always resolve problems – do not simply hope they will go away, because they will not and they are likely to have got worse in the meantime.

Health and safety at work

What is health and safety at work about? Everyone has responsibilities under the Health and Safety at Work Act (HASAWA) – employers, employees and people (customers) using the establishment.

Every employee has a legal responsibility to:

- Ensure reasonable care for his/her health and safety
- Ensure that colleagues and other people are not adversely affected by his/her omissions (things they have not done)
- Cooperate with the employers to meet health and safety requirements
- Ensure that he/she does not interfere with anything or misuse anything provided in the interests of health and safety. (This also applies to employers.)

Employers are also responsible for maintaining a safe working environment. All employers must ensure the health, safety and welfare of their employees and other people as far as is reasonably possible.

The employer's responsibilities are under six headings:

1 Provide safe equipment and safe ways of carrying out jobs.
2 Ensure that the use, handling, storage and transport of everything is safe and without risks to health.
3 Provide information, instruction, training and supervision to ensure health and safety.
4 Provide a safe workplace, including safe entries (ways of getting in) and exits (ways of getting out) of the workplace.
5 Provide a safe working environment with adequate facilities.
6 Write a safety policy.

In practice, this means that there are certain areas of concern:

- Fire procedures
- Suspicious packages
- Accident procedures
- Ensuring a safe and secure environment for customers, staff and visitors.

Fire procedures

Task 3.53

Walk round your workplace, school, college, sports centre, etc., noting down the position of fire extinguishers and any other fire-fighting equipment.

Beside each item explain how you would use it and what you would use it for.

As you have found out, there are lots of different fire extinguishers for different types of fire. For example, you must not use a water extinguisher on a fat fire because oil floats on water and the fire would spread.

Figure 3.10 shows examples of different types of fire fighting equipment.

Task 3.54

What should you do when you hear a fire alarm? How should you leave the building?

Put together a list of fire rules for evacuating the building safely.

How would you make sure customers knew the procedures? How would you make sure everyone was out?
Element 3.4, PC4

Suspicious packages

Task 3.55

What sort of examples are included under the heading 'suspicious packages'?

If you find a suspicious parcel or package, DO NOT TOUCH IT. Inform security or your supervisor and follow their instructions.

When you arrive at work, always have a look around. Check for objects that are in the wrong place or any suspicious objects.

Figure 3.10

Task 3.56

What should you do if you receive a bomb threat phone call? Make a list of procedures.
Element 3.4, PC4

1 Stay calm and try to keep the caller talking for as long as possible. Listen to the voice for an accent or for any background clues. Ask questions.

2 When the caller hangs up:

 – dial 999 for the police
 – inform your supervisor
 – follow the procedure for an emergency.

Accident procedures

Task 3.57

Find out what you should do in the event of an accident at:

● *The place where you are studying this course*
● *The local swimming pool*
● *A sports hall.*

Make general notes about the procedures you should follow. Find out who is responsible for first aid and what their responsibilities are.
Element 3.4, PC4

Everyone who has an accident should complete an accident report form.

Task 3.58

On Wednesday January 17th you slipped over in the changing room of the leisure centre and hit your head on a bench. When you were taken to hospital, you needed three stitches in the cut on your forehead.

Michael Livingstone, who saw you slip, called a First Aider who comforted you, bathed your head and gave you a lint compress to hold against it.

Complete the following accident report form with the details of this accident.

ACCIDENT REPORT FORM

Name of injured person:

Address:

Telephone number:

Date of accident:

Where did the accident happen?

What was the cause?

Details of injuries:

Details of First Aid given:

Name of hospital:

Treatment received:

Signature:　　　　*Date:*

Element 3.4, PC4

Ensuring a safe and secure working environment

Task 3.59	Task 3.60

Look carefully at the illustration and make a list of the hazards or potential hazards, explain why they are dangerous and detail what action needs to be taken.

Choose one of these hazards. Find out who you should report it to and then leave a clear message for him/her:

● *Outline the hazard*
● *Explain its location*
● *Explain why it is dangerous.*

Some of the hazards or potential hazards you have identified will be the employer's responsibility to correct.

Apart from a safe environment, customers also expect secure surroundings.

Figure 3.11

Task 3.61

Find out about the security policy at your place of work, school or college.

There should also be a procedure for recording missing items reported by customers.

Task 3.62

Mrs Brown has booked a squash court. At the end of the game, she returns to the changing rooms only to find the locker has been broken into and items have been stolen.

Take down details of the missing items and record them in the lost property book. (You have to devise the document to include all necessary details.)
Element 3.4, PC4

Summary

The health and safety of yourself, customers and anyone else in the building is very important. Hopefully, you are now familiar with standard procedures for dealing with potentially dangerous situations, although different companies will have different policies. It is important you become familiar with routines to deal with fire, suspicious parcels and accidents.

▪ Assignment 3.4 ▪

Being able to deal with customers is very important and finding out what they really want is a skill.

Scenario

Through the role-play situation you are going to find out what three different customers actually need and then you are going to assess how you think you have done.

Details

1 You are working on the reception area of a sports complex. Throughout the morning you will be dealing with some very different customers.
2 You will be asked to deal with three customers to the best of your ability.
3 You will also be expected to keep relevant records of the incidents for you to pass to either your supervisor (if necessary) or to a colleague who is to replace you at the end of your shift.
4 How do you think you got on? Could you have improved in any way? How would you change your approach if a similar situation arose again?

RUNNING AN EVENT

Planning an event

This section looks at the important features involved in organizing events. It also looks at different types of event and why they are staged. It explores decisions that have been made prior to the planning of an event.

Events

Events form a significant section of the leisure and tourism industry. Throughout history events have been an important feature of people's lives. Many of these revolved around religious festivals and cultural and sporting events. One of the biggest events today, the Olympic Games, has its roots firmly in the past. The Games were was first held in 776 BC by the Greeks and have now developed into an international event with countries keenly competing for the right to host them, due to the prestige and potential income they can generate.

Nowadays events are not necessarily staged on special occasions. They can be used by the industry for a specific purpose, for example to generate income or to attract new customers.

What are events?

Events are special occasions which are different from the usual run of the mill activities that we are involved with in our everyday lives. They are highlights that often linger for many years in the memories of people.

Task 4.1

Ask an older person what special events they remember from their childhood. Report these back to the rest of your group. Try to write a brief account of the event from the details that have been given to you.

Element 4.1, PC3

When we think about events, large major events immediately spring to mind, for example the World Cup Soccer Finals, or the World Chess Championships. However, the nature of events that take place within the leisure and tourism industry are extremely diverse – from, for example, a local dog show to the London Marathon.

Table 4.1

Local	Regional	National	International
School summer fête	Special exhibition at a museum	Last night of the Proms	Olympic Games

---

Task 4.2

Make a list of all the special events you have either heard of, seen on television or read about in the newspapers. Table 4.1 shows how you might present your list.
Element 4.1, PC3

You will notice from the list that you have made that some of these events are local, for example the school summer fête, others are regional, for example a special exhibition, others are national, for example the last night of the Proms, while others are international, for example the Olympic Games.

Having looked at the diverse nature of special events in the leisure and tourism industry, we shall now consider the reasons for organizing these events.

Why organize events?

The reasons for staging events are, just like the nature of events themselves, very diverse and can include some of the following:
● To raise a profit
● To increase visitor numbers to a particular event
● For enjoyment
● To improve facilities (Sheffield is an excellent example of this after hosting the World Student Games)
● To promote a worthwhile cause, e.g. a local hospice
● To introduce new activities/products to people
● To increase/affect participation, for example to increase participation in sport by women in the community
● To promote the cultural heritage of an area/ country, for example the Highland Games.

When organizing an event the objective, i.e. what you want to achieve by the event, should be clearly understood by all those who are involved in it so that all the team are working towards the same target. Having established the objective of the event, plans should be made to achieve it. The objective must be achievable and realistic: for example, if the local church summer fête aimed to raise one million pounds the chances of achieving this would be very small indeed.

Task 4.3

Read the article 'Sky high success' (Figure 4.1), which is a report by a local Hoylake & West Kirby newspaper about a lifeboat day in Hoylake in the Wirral. When you have read the article, answer the following questions:

- *Why was this event staged?*
- *What was its main objective?*
- *Was this a local, regional, national or international event? Give reasons for your answers.*
- *List features of the event that attracted the crowd.*
- *What was the main attraction that had been arranged to encourage people to attend?*
- *Carole Jackson, the organizer of this event, was employed by Wirral WBC Leisure and Tourism Department. Can you think of some reasons why Wirral WBC may support this event?*
- *List any problems that occurred and suggest how these could have been overcome.*
- *Do you think that the organizers were successful in achieving their aims? Give your reasons.*
Element 4.1, PC2 and 6

SPECTACULAR *Traffic at a standstill as town is besieged for annual Lifeboat Open Day*

SKY HIGH SUCCESS!

Show was 'best ever' say delighted organisers
by Helen Wakefield

AEROBATIC daredevils the Red Arrows brought West Wirral to a standstill at what has been hailed the biggest and best lifeboat open day ever!

The Bank Holiday sunshine and a packed programme of free entertainment brought out a record 30,000 people and raised a massive £17,000 topping last year's figure of £15,000.

The show got off to a "cracker" of a start with comedian Frank Carson, who received an RNLI flag parachuted in by the Pegasus Parachute Team.

Jazz and brass bands plus the Berliner Beatles brought a musical note to the open day held annually at Hoylake Lifeboat Station.

A surprise appearance from colleagues at RAF Valley, Anglesey with the familiar yellow Wessex helicopter delighted the crowds.

For many people it was a great chance to see the lifeboats at close quarters, and thousands ventured aboard the Lady of Hilbre, where the crew was on hand to chat with visitors.

Chairman of Hoylake and West Kirby Lifeboat Station and organiser, Mr Stan Frith said: "It was the biggest and best lifeboat open day without a doubt."

Organiser Carole Jackson said: "It put Hoylake on the map as we spoke to people from as far as Yorkshire.

"The Red Arrows were absolutely breathtaking and I'm wondering if there's anything we can do next year to make it even better."

A mass exodus of visitors at the end of the show brought chaos to Market Street.

Chief Inspector Ronnie Garnett said: "We felt the day went very well. At the end we were snowed under with traffic but it's to be expected with something like the Red Arrows and Hoylake's narrow streets."

Figure 4.1

Most events are organized through good team (two or more persons working together) work. It is important that when tasks are allocated within a team the strengths of its members are put to good use. For example, it is no good asking someone to be treasurer who is very poor with figures. The following is a list of roles that can be adopted in an event:

● Coordinator
● Secretary
● Treasurer
● Marketing/promotion.

Obviously the number in the team and their responsibilities will vary according to the scale of the event.

Task 4.4

List the characteristics required for each of the four roles described. Table 4.2 shows how you might present your list.
Element 4.2, PC7

It is important that all the team members fully understand what their jobs entail and are aware of all the schedules and deadlines that have been agreed. It is much better to have someone

Table 4.2

Coordinator	Secretary	Treasurer	Promotions Officer
Good leadership qualities	Good communication skills	Good with figures	Artistic

in your team who is reliable, rather than a 'prima donna' who promises everything and delivers nothing!

In order to stage an event, a comprehensive list of resources should be made well in advance of the event so that necessary steps can be taken to make sure that they are acquired in good time. You may be able to get help with these through sponsorship from local firms and help may be provided by local organizations and charities. At Wimbledon the ball boys and girls are recruited from local schools. Once all the necessary resources have been obtained they should be checked to ensure that they work, are safe and are suitable for the job intended. When resources are booked or hired it is very important to keep accurate records – always confirm in writing. Anything that has been borrowed should be returned promptly after the event, otherwise next time this source may be withdrawn. Always remember to thank, in writing, any contributors to the event – you may wish to ask them again and goodwill should always be fostered.

When organizing an event every eventuality should be planned for. For example, fire escapes must be in place. Also, planners should consider possible disruptions to their event. If you are staging a garden party, what has been organized in the event of rain? It is important to have a clear plan of action in case things go wrong so that this plan can be executed with minimal disruption to the event should problems arise. If the staff have practised these plans then they should be able to be put them into operation swiftly and effectively.

When all features of the event have been considered, a detailed plan for the event can be formulated. In this plan all features of the event should be covered with time-scales set and closely monitored to make sure that everything runs to schedule. After the event has been staged the team should meet to discuss whether the event was successful and to what extent objectives were met. Features that went well and problems that occurred should be highlighted so that these can be taken into consideration next time.

Remember, planning is of vital importance in any event. If you fail to plan your event may fail, and nobody wants to attend an event that is a failure. In this section we have considered:

- Features of events
- Categories of events
- Why events are organized
- Teamwork planning
- Responsibilities within the team
- Resources
- Contingencies
- Monitoring schedules
- Reviewing the event.

In the next section we will look in more detail at how roles in an event are undertaken.

• Assignment 4.1 •

You have been asked to organize a day out for a group of old age pensioners. Select a suitable venue or itinerary. Remember, you will need to arrange a midday lunch for the party. Undertake the following:

1 List the objectives of the visit and planning stages leading up to the visit.
2 Include sample letters, booking/confirmation, etc., and different services entailed within the visit, e.g. coach, lunch.
3 Produce a statement of account that you will use to calculate the cost of the visit.
4 Highlight contingency plans that could be incorporated in your plan.
5 Identify the roles that need to be undertaken in order to distribute the work involved in the event.
6 Allocate these roles according to the strengths of your team.

Planning contributions to a team event

As we have seen in the first section, most events are not the result of one person's work alone. They are the united effort of a group of people, or a team, who are all working for the same objective, that is to achieve a successful event. Within this team there will be a number of people who have different skills and strengths and weaknesses in their areas of work. These skills and strengths and weaknesses should be considered carefully when the various jobs within the team are allocated.

In this section we are going to look at a team that is involved in organizing an event. We will then look at the individual contributions that are to be made for the overall event to be staged. Each team member will plan their own contribution to the event to be staged. We will consider:

● How one person's role in an event can support another's and can support the objectives of the event
● How by adopting certain methods the resources available can be used to their maximum benefit
● How roles are undertaken with a consideration for health, safety and security
● How roles are carried out in such a way as to promote goodwill
● What a person should do when something happens and their role does not go to plan
● Problems that may occur and how they could be handled effectively to try to reduce their impact on the event
● How staff and customers can be informed promptly and clearly of any changes which may affect them
● General guidelines for undertaking a role in an event.

Roles and responsibilities of the team

One of the first things that has to be done before the event team can proceed is for officers, or jobs, to be appointed. These officers could work on their own, though, for a large event, they would probably work as part of a separate team or committee. For example, a finance officer may work within a finance committee.

The first officer to be appointed in the organizing team or committee would be the Chairperson or **Coordinator**. This is probably the most important person in the whole event as it is this person who oversees the entire event and makes sure that all the jobs necessary are done within the agreed time-scale. Their responsibilities would include:

● Overview of the event
● Liaison with other members of the team
● Ensuring that all jobs are completed
● Ensuring that deadlines are met
● Raising any problems that may be occurring and finding solutions
● Chairing meetings of the event committee
● Ensuring that everyone has a fair share of time to raise issues, voice opinions, etc. at meetings
● Making sure that order is kept in the meeting without little sub-groups being formed to discuss side issues
● Making sure that the agenda for the meeting is covered
● If decisions cannot be reached through discussion a vote on an issue may be taken. The coordinator organizes this and, in the event of an equal number of votes being cast for and against an issue, has the right to use a casting vote to decide on the outcome.

The role of the coordinator is a very difficult one. There may be occasions when the coordinator receives complaints from a variety of different sources and these have to be dealt with as tactfully as possible.

Task 4.5

The coordinator of a Rugby Sevens tournament has received a complaint from a member of the organizing committee. The local rugby club where his brother is a member has been invited to play in the competition for the last ten years but has not received an invitation this year. Describe the action that the coordinator could take in response to this complaint.
Element 4.2, PC4

Once a coordinator has been appointed, other officers will be decided upon. If more than one person is proposed for a job then a vote will be taken. The coordinator would organize this vote.

An **Administrator** will be appointed. Their responsibilities would include:

● Dealing with correspondence/letters etc.
● Producing minutes of the committee meetings (these are a record of what has been said, what has been decided and who is to do what before the next meeting). These would be circulated to all members prior to the next meeting.
● Assisting other members of the team with administrative procedures.

Task 4.6

The administrator of a local charitable organization, planning a fireworks display on November 5th, has just received a letter from the First Aid organization who had agreed to be present at the event, one week before the event, to say that they are overbooked and unfortunately cannot send a representative. Describe the action the administrator may take in response to this letter.
Element 4.2, PC1, 2, 4, 6 and 7

A Treasurer or **Financial Controller** will be appointed. Their responsibilities would include:

● Overseeing all financial transactions
● Recording financial transactions
● Holding the cheque book (if one exists)
● Setting up a secure system of using the money available, e.g. designating two people – one of whom may be the financial controller – who are jointly responsible for signing and authorizing payments
● Producing an income/expenditure account, with receipts etc. clearly documented
● Designing procedures for the secure holding of income, before, during and after the event
● *Ensuring that the team meets the budget set.*

Task 4.7

A local hotel is organizing a Valentine's Supper Dance. The aim of this event is to promote the hotel's restaurant facilities and make a fair profit of 40 per cent. The overall cost to the hotel when everything has been accounted for is £1,200 based on two hundred attending. How much would the tickets be sold for in order to meet the financial targets of the event?
Element 4.3, PC1

A **Publicity Officer** will be appointed. Their responsibilities would include:

● Promoting the event
● Organizing promotional materials (adverts, leaflets, etc.) according to the scale of the event
● Liaising with outside agencies, e.g. local newspaper companies, radio stations
● Organizing press coverage of the event, e.g. arrangements could be made for a photographer from the local paper to attend.

Task 4.8

A local fitness club is holding a special event for non-members promoting the facilities and courses available. They are particularly targeting women between the ages of 20 and 30:

1 *Design an advert that promotes this event.*
2 *State where it would appear and give reasons for your choice.*
   Element 4.1, PC2, 5 and 7

A **Catering Officer** could be appointed, depending on the nature of the event. Their responsibilities may include:

- Providing hospitality services for the guests, staff and VIPs
- Ordering all food/drink/catering equipment
- Hygiene
- Organizing catering team members
- Overseeing preparation of food and drink etc.
- Clearing up of dishes etc., during and after the event.

Task 4.9

A local travel agent is holding an event to promote the refurbishment of their office. As Catering Officer for the event, decide what you will need to provide for customers and invited guests.
Element 4.2, PC1, 2, 3, 4 and 7

A **Facility Officer** will be appointed. Their responsibilities may include:

- Finding and organizing the venue
- Organizing specialist equipment for the event, e.g. lighting

- Security arrangements
- Parking arrangements
- Toilet facilities
- Obtaining and displaying appropriate signs
- Ensuring adequate access into and around the building.

Task 4.10

The Facility Officer for a local drama group has been asked to find a venue to stage their Christmas pantomime. Research the venues available in your locality. State which venues are available and which would be the one that you would recommend to the group. Give reasons for your choice.
Element 4.2, PC1, 2, 3 and 7

Although members of the event team all have particular responsibilities, it is important that all members are able to communicate effectively so that problems can be highlighted and dealt with as effectively as possible.

Task 4.11

The people listed in Figure 4.2 are the members of an event committee. However, specific responsibilities have not as yet been allocated.

Read the list of officers again from the descriptions of the six members of the committee and decide who would be best suited for each of these positions. Give reasons for your choice. Table 4.3 shows how you might present your list.
Element 4.1, PC7

John is very reliable and always gives his work in on time. His work is well presented with excellent use of presentations. In his spare time he runs his own disco

Michelle is confident and extrovert. She mixes with lots of different groups in college and is very popular. She is used to dealing with money as she has a part-time job at a local restaurant where her father is the chef

Helen is a well organized and confident student. She is not afraid to express her opinions, even if they do not always agree with the rest of the group. When Helen works in a group situation she is always the first to take the lead and often offers helpful, positive suggestions on how problems should be solved

Paul is quite shy when mixing with the rest of the group. He is well organized in his work and has a really clear way of wording his assignments. The way he puts something always sounds good! He is an enthusiastic PC user and often helps other members of the team when they are stuck

Mark runs a local market stall at weekends. It is his own business. He does not have a large turnover but he keeps careful records so that they can be looked at if necessary

Jane is well organized, quiet yet confident. She has a part-time job as a receptionist at a local hotel, so she is used to dealing with customers' complaints

Figure 4.2

Table 4.3

Name	Position	Reason for choice

Each of the officers listed can if required form their own team or committee in order to complete their necessary tasks. The scale and scope of this will obviously depend on the nature of the event. An administrator for the London Marathon would have a much larger team than an administrator for a local village fête.

What happens next?

When all the officers have been appointed the committee must meet to plan their overall event strategy. They will probably cover some or all of the following at this stage:

- Why do we want to hold this event?
- What are our objectives – what do we want to achieve?
- Who are we aiming this event at – i.e. who do we want to come?
- When is the best time to hold the event?
- Where is the best place to hold the event?
- How much will it cost to stage?
- How much would people be prepared to pay to attend the event?
- Do we want to raise money, i.e. make a profit, or are we just doing this to cover costs?
- A time-scale of how different tasks will be planned and implemented.
- The need for good team effort, sticking to budgets and using resources available to their best advantage.
- Efficient uses of communication between members.
- Effective publicity.
- Contingency plans.
- Strategy for dealing with customers.

- A good working environment: friendly, supportive, etc.
- Feedback to all contributors on the outcome of the event.

Once the overall strategy has been decided, each team can plan their particular jobs with the overall aim of the event in view.

Case study

John, Jane, Michelle, Helen, Paul and Mark are members of a GNVQ Intermediate Leisure & Tourism group. They have all been allocated a specific responsibility (see Task 4.11). The group has been approached by a representative from a Parent Teacher Association from a local school. They have taken on too much and would like the group to stage an event they have planned. This event is a Sale of Nearly New Toys, which is an annual pre-Christmas event. This gives parents the opportunity to sell nearly new toys to others. As the school takes a percentage of the prices of the toys sold and charges an admission fee to this event, it means that the school makes a good income for school funds too.

Task 4.12

The committee meets to set out their objectives for this event. Write a brief report on what you think these objectives will be.
Element 4.1, PC2

When the overall aim for the event has been agreed, other decisions have to be made before individuals can proceed with tasks which are their responsibility.

Task 4.13

Look back at the text. Using the information provided, state what decisions the committee has to take before individual officers plan their contribution to the overall event.
Element 4.1, PC1, 2, 3, 4, 5 and 7

Coordinator

- Liaises with committee members
- Liaises with school caretakers
- Gives assistance to committee members as required
- Communicates vital information to the team
- Oversees that all tasks are running to the schedules
- Ensures that enough helpers are recruited to cover all aspects of the event.

Administrator

- Sends a letter to parents with details of the event well in advance so that they can prepare
- Ensures that reminders appear in regular newsletters about forthcoming events
- Designs a form to be used by those selling toys detailing:
  - Name of seller
  - Address
  - Toys for sale
  - Brief description
  - Price to be set
- Devises a labelling system that can be used to sell the toys and to check back against the original sales form
- Sends a letter to parents with appropriate forms for the sale of toys and outlining all necessary arrangements
- Sends a letter after the event to thank the helpers
- Sends a letter to all members of the PTA Committee and parents informing them of the profit made.

Finance Officer

- Decides on the amount needed to use as a float for the sale of the toys (i.e the money that is to be used to give the buyers change)
- Decides how this money should be broken down, i.e. how many £5, £1, 50p, 20p, 10p, 5p, 2p, 1p
- Decides on how many different floats should be made
- Obtains money for the catering on the advice of the Catering Officer, to include a float and money needed to purchase foodstuffs etc.
- Writes out a cheque from the account and obtains a second signature
- Arranges collection of entry fee
- Goes to the bank to cash the cheque
- Stores this money in a secure place on the advice of the Facility Officer
- Organizes regular emptying of cash from points of sale to a secure place
- Arranges for payment of appropriate amounts to sellers of toys
- Arranges for sellers to sign for the money they have received
- Arranges for a percentage to be calculated from each sale
- Records income from sales
- Records income from refreshments
- Produces a Statement of Account
- Arranges for safe storage of profits.

Facility Officer

- Looks at the venue and decides whereabouts in the school the sale will take place
- Researches regulations, e.g. the number of people allowed in the space allocated for the sale
- Checks the fire exits – ensures that they are working properly and have not been obstructed
- Checks fire extinguishers
- Checks fire blankets in the kitchen area
- Organizes tables to be set up for the toys to be displayed

- Produces a plan for tables to be arranged for the sale of toys and for the refreshment area
- Allocates space for sellers to receive their money
- Organizes unsold toys to be grouped by the seller so that they can be collected and removed
- Considers the health and safety aspects of, for example, carrying hot drinks and movement of customers
- Oversees security, and recruits helpers to oversee purchases
- Plans a system to identify which toys have been paid for to help with security.

Catering Officer

- Obtains a budget from the Finance Officer
- Decides on light refreshments
- Purchases items needed
- Recruits helpers
- Arranges for equipment to be made available
- Displays notices of refreshments available and prices
- Ensures that tables have cloths and look attractive
- Organizes clearing of tables
- Organizes the washing-up team
- Oversees the final clearing up of the catering area
- Briefs helpers about hygiene in the kitchen.

Publicity Officer

- Obtains a budget from the Finance Officer for promotional material
- Designs an advert for the local paper
- Organizes the advert to appear in the local paper
- Organizes a note reminding local residents of the events
- Recruits a team of helpers to deliver these notes
- Designs posters for local shop/house windows

- Arranges for all promotional material to be printed
- Arranges for all promotional material to be displayed
- Arranges for the local newspaper to take a photo of the event.

Once all the tasks have been identified, an action plan can be produced by each of the officers which will show clearly what is to be achieved by when.

As part of your course you will be asked to contribute to an event with others. We will now look at roles undertaken in an event and show situations which may arise that can affect a person's role.

Case study

A small group of students have been asked to work as a group and produce an exhibition of the local leisure and tourism facilities in their locality. This exhibition is to be used for an Open Day being held at the college to publicize the facilities and courses available. There are three members of the group.

Task 4.14

Decide when the event is to be staged and at what time. Using the task list of each officer, complete Table 4.4. showing how each task is scheduled to fit in with the overall event. Use a separate page for each officer. You may decide that for the day of the event you need a precise timing record.
Element 4.2, PC1, 2, 3, 4 and 7

Task 4.15

Make a plan of all the things that they need to do to complete this task. Decide how they might share the work out. Indicate how they could help each other to obtain a good overall result.
Element 4.1, PC1, 2, 5, 6, 7 and 8
Element 4.2, PC1, 2, 3, 4 and 7

Table 4.4

Officer	Tasks weeks before event					After event	
	8	6	4	2	1	1	2
Coordinator							
Administrator							
Finance Officer							
Publicity Officer							
Catering Officer							
Facility Officer							

Figure 4.3 An exhibition stand

The team has worked well together. They have obtained the material they need and have started to organize it on the stand. One of the team has printed notices out at home on her printer. However, the quality is very poor and the other members of the team do not think that it is good enough to be displayed on the stand.

Task 4.16

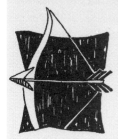

Suggest ways that the team could deal with this problem. Are there any facilities available in their college to improve these notices? If so, state what they are (be realistic) and show how the team could make good use of them.

Element 4.2, PC2 and 4

On the day of the event the various stands that are located in the entrance hall take up more space than was previously indicated. The area that the group has been allocated for their stand partially obstructs a fire exit.

Task 4.17

What action if any should the group take? Who could they go to for help and advice?
Element 4.2, PC1, 2, 3 and 7

Due to the problem of space some of the stands have covered important notices that are on the walls. One of the stands covers a no smoking sign – there should have been a no smoking sign on the entrance door but it has blown away in the wind. Someone enters the hall and lights up a cigarette.

Task 4.18

Describe what action the three members of the group should take. Try to act out your response – if you have a video camera available, record your actions so that you can watch afterwards to see if the problem was handled correctly. Describe how the three of you divide the responses that have to be made to this problem.
Element 4.2, PC1, 2, 3, 4, 6 and 7

During the event a manager of a local fitness centre arrives to view your exhibition stand. He studies it in detail and then starts to complain, very loudly, that his particular organization has not been featured in the display.

Task 4.19

Detail what your reaction may be to this customer. Remember, goodwill is vital – you may meet this person in the future on work experience.
Element 4.2, PC6 and 7

The rooms used in the event are spread out over a wide area. People have been positioned at key places to welcome guests on arrival and to help direct them to the areas they wish to visit. There is one

person available in the entrance hall where your group's stand is located. However, this person is looking very hot and bothered and there is a queue waiting to ask for directions. Your stand is not particularly busy and you do not really need three people to be present.

Task 4.20

Suggest how you could help overcome this problem.
Element 4.2, PC1, 2, 3, 4, 5, 6 and 7

During the evening someone slips on the stairs and hurts their ankle very badly. The First Aider is called and she decides that the injured person, who is in considerable pain, should not be moved and that an ambulance must be called.

Task 4.21

The facility in which the event is taking place has a lift which serves all floors. Describe what action the event organizer could take in response to the injured person both at the location of the accident and outside the building. Detail what the organizer should do once the injured person has been removed from the scene of the accident.
Element 4.2, PC4, 6 and 7

As part of the event, light snacks and drinks have been offered for sale at a small cost in the dining area of the school/college. The foodstuffs are perishable and cannot be frozen. Towards the end of the evening, due to the large amount of food left over, it is decided that it should be offered to staff and visitors free of charge. However, this information must be relayed to them as soon as possible before they all start to leave.

Task 4.22

How can this information be given to staff and visitors as quickly as possible? What effect will this policy have on future events of this nature?
Element 4.2, PC2, 4, 6 and 7

As can be seen by the examples illustrated, an individual can plan their role in an event in great detail. However, quite frequently something happens which disrupts the event and responses have to be made as quickly and efficiently as possible.

It has not been unusual for major events to be disrupted for a variety of different reasons, for example someone crossing the racecourse at Ascot, or a protest against something occurring.

Task 4.23

Give an explanation of why major events may be interrupted by protesters or exhibitionists. What response have the media made to these disruptions?
Element 4.2, PC6

There are occasions when major events have been disrupted not by protesters or intruders, but by key aspects of the organization of the event going wrong.

Task 4.24

Research what happened in the 1993 Grand National – you could do this by looking at old newspapers which reported the event (your library will keep them or you may find them in a database) or ask your family and friends what happened. Write a brief report on how one person's role in an event attracted the attention of the world's media.
Element 4.2, PC4 and 6

Undertaking a role in an event can be very stressful: some positions carry a great deal of responsibility. If each individual plans their duties well and to time, then unless something totally unforeseen occurs the event should run smoothly. It is important in any event for the organizers to keep calm so that any necessary responses can be made as quickly and efficiently as possible.

General guidelines for events

- *Be prepared*   As the Scout motto says! Good preparation is the foundation for a good event. If the team as a whole are well prepared this will set the tone for the event.
- *Be clear about your objectives*   Make sure that all the team fully understand what is to be achieved by the staging of this event. If all team members are well informed, everyone will be working towards the same goal.
- *Work as a team*   Any good team builds on the strengths of its members and is supportive and helpful to each other. To operate effectively the team should meet on a regular basis and be able to communicate with each other with relative ease. A good team has a good team leader at its front. This team leader should be a good motivator who can generate enthusiasm and perseverance.
- *Remember customer care*   A smile of welcome costs nothing and will affect the way

visitors feel about the event. Remember, even if your stand/job in the event isn't very busy do not sit around looking bored and uninterested – this is sure to put potential clients off. Try to be alert, ready for action and enthusiastic at all times. If clients enjoy the event they will come back and tell their friends.

- *Be recognizable* More and more teams in organizations are adopting their own uniforms. These help the visitors as it makes the staff immediately recognizable from the clients. When you stage an event you should consider adopting a uniform for all the staff involved in the event. This does not have to be complicated or expensive. For example, the team may decide to wear black trousers and a white T-shirt. These are items of clothing that most people have in their wardrobes. Plain coloured T-shirts are relatively inexpensive to purchase. You may have the facilities at your school/college to print the name of your event on the front, or a local screen

printer would do this at a small cost. This creates a good image for the visitors of the event and is something the rest of the team can keep to remind them of the event in the future.

- *Keep to schedules* Reliability, both within the team and within the event itself, is important. The team should make sure that all deadlines are met if it is at all possible to do so. Punctuality should be important for all team meetings etc. If someone is always late for a meeting it is unsurprising that other team members act on their knowledge and turn up, not at the start time or before, but at the time that they think the meeting will begin. This can lead to frayed tempers and much wasted time. Remember, on the day of the event make sure that the event team arrives in good time in order to set up all the necessary equipment etc. A rehearsal is a good way of checking for problems in organization and for monitoring the time needed for the event to be put in place. Allow more than the time you took in the rehearsal as things could still go wrong. It is much better to have time for a sit down and a cup of coffee before visitors arrive, than to be still setting up equipment after the event has started. Try to keep your event running to schedule – visitors organize themselves around this schedule and problems can occur if timings go drastically wrong.

- *Keep accurate records* Always keep minutes of your event team meetings. Minutes have a clear structure and are usually taken by the secretary or administrator. Minutes should be circulated to each committee member before each committee meeting so that everyone has been informed of the discussion that occurred at the previous meeting and what is to be covered by the next meeting. At one end of the minutes it is good practice to include a summary of outcomes and action points. The outcomes cover things that have been decided and things that need doing. Actions refer to who is to make sure that the outcome is achieved.

Figure 4.4

Leighton Lawn Tennis Club
Ground Wimbledon Road, Leighton
Minutes of the Social Committee Meeting
held on Thursday 22 September 1994

Present: Jayne Fisher (Chair)
           Rob Gold
           Barbara Fosdyke
           Mike Denton
           Julie McKenna (Secretary)

1 Apologies for absence were received from John Davies and Jill Smith.

2 The minutes of the last meeting held on 21 July 1994 were accepted as a true record.

3 Matters Arising

3.1   J Fisher reported the progress with the kitchen improvement. Quotes will be obtained from a number of kitchen companies as soon as possible to establish who will carry out the work.

3.2   Sweets left over from the summer tournament will be used at a forthcoming event.

4 Ordinary Business

4.1   The Autumn/Winter social programme was discussed. It was decided to hold a Barn Dance and to include a light supper. R Gold will find a venue and then arrange a date for this depending upon venue availability. The weekend of November 26th was considered to be most suitable since after this date people may be involved in Christmas functions. Once the date has been fixed B Forsdyke will book a band and M Denton will apply for a bar licence via the local magistrates court if the venue selected does not have its own bar, and will obtain menus and then book a caterer. A small supper, e.g. vegetable chilli, was thought to be appropriate. J Fisher will get the tickets printed and will produce a publicity letter for this event that will be distributed to all members via J McKenna's teams of helpers. Progress to be reported at next meeting.

4.2   J Fisher suggested a possible event for February – a Murder Mystery Meal. She will obtain details for this event and will report back at the next meeting.

5 Any Other Business

J McKenna reported on plans to take a group of junior members to a local pantomime in December.

6 Date of Next Meeting

Thursday 8 December at 7.45 pm.

Outcomes	Action points
Kitchen improvements	J Fisher to obtain three quotes from kitchen companies
Left over sweets to be sold	B Fosdyke to sell these at the next club tournament
Barn Dance venue required	R Gold to find a suitable venue and set the date for the event
Arrangements for the band	B Fosdyke to book band
Application for bar licence and caterers	M Denton to apply via Magistrates Court for licence. Book caterers
Organize tickets and publicity	J Fisher
Distribution of tickets	J McKenna and team
Research Murder Mystery Event	J Fisher

Task 4.25

Read the Minutes of the Social Committee for Leighton Tennis Club who are holding a Barn Dance for members and friends. Look at what has been decided and needs to be done for this event. List these under Outcomes. Then look at who is to do what and by when, and list these under Actions. You could set your answer out as shown in Table 4.5.
Element 4.2, PC1, 2, 3 and 4

Minutes of meetings should be carefully stored using an appropriate method so that club members or the committee members can refer back to issues that have been discussed and action that has been decided.

When organizing an event it is vitally important that all necessary bookings etc. are confirmed in writing and a copy kept for the file. A fax machine is a very quick and useful method of communication – you are also able to keep the copy of the message you have sent. Keep the report it gives you to say that the

message has been transmitted and received in full. These receipts, like other documentation, can be very useful if a problem occurs, e.g. a venue is double-booked. Good communication is important, not only with external organizations, but with the committee itself. All committee members should be kept informed of the organization of the event as it progresses.

The Finance Officer has a particular responsibility to produce an accurate record of accounts and to present these as required.

If all roles in an event are undertaken efficiently, success will be guaranteed. The visitors will enjoy the event and will tell their friends and will want to attend another similar event in the future. This is a good foundation for the preparation of the next event.

In this section we have looked at how roles are undertaken in an event and have considered general guidelines which will help organizers in an event to undertake their particular post/role as successfully as possible.

In the next section we will consider what happens after the event has been staged – the review and evaluation of the event itself.

Table 4.5

Outcomes	Action

▪ Assignment 4.2 ▪

1 You will undertake an event with the rest of your group. During this event keep a log recording your own contribution to the overall team event. If you have a video camera you may like to video your contribution. Ask one of the other members of the team to observe your contribution and write a report. Does your assessment of your contribution agree with that of the observer? If not, how do the assessments differ?

2 You are holding a disco for your group at a local venue. A disruption occurs. Select the disruption that takes place and write a report on the nature of the disruption and the action taken to overcome the problem.

Evaluating the event

In the last section we looked at how roles are undertaken in an event. In this section we are going to consider how and why events are evaluated – by evaluation we mean the response or feedback from all those involved in the event. We will be looking at:

● The purpose of the evaluation
● The importance of evaluation to any event
● The process of evaluation
● The effects of feedback on the needs of the team
● How future events can be affected.

Evaluation of any event is concerned with the feedback from the event – not just from those who organized or staffed the event, but from anyone who played a part in it. This could include:

● Staff
● Organizers
● Clients/visitors
● Volunteers
● Cleaners
● Sponsors
● Officials.

Why evaluate an event?

When an event is planned, the purpose of the event is clearly defined. It is against this that the event should be evaluated. Evaluation does not just take place at the end of an event. It is an ongoing process which occurs throughout the event. During the planning stage everything to do with the event is monitored and if any problems appear adjustments have to be made. It is through this process that the event is finally staged and organized to meet the objectives of the event.

It is important to stand back and consider the event, as sometimes during the event things have been so hectic that organizers have little time for considering whether targets etc. are being met. This opportunity to review and evaluate the event is important as a learning exercise. If the event is to be staged again in the future it is an invaluable help as the things that went well can be repeated, while those things that were not too successful can be changed next time. Furthermore, events need a lot of time and effort putting into them. If the event is a failure, this has been a waste of valuable resources – time and effort, not to mention any financial resources that may have been needed to stage the event. When you undertake an event in your group at school/college, make sure that you prepare a full report on the evaluation of your event. Highlight the particular problems that you encountered and how you overcame them. This will be an invaluable help to the group who follow you next year – they will be able to learn from your mistakes!

Case study

The Social Committee of the Tennis Club meet to review the Barn Dance. Minutes of the meeting are shown overleaf. The aim of the Barn Dance was to:

● Sell 100 tickets
● Give an enjoyable evening to members
● Make a profit for club funds.

Leighton Lawn Tennis Club
Ground Wimbledon Road, Leighton
Minutes of the Social Committee Meeting
held on Thursday 8 December 1994

Present:　Jayne Fisher (Chair)
　　　　　Rob Gold
　　　　　Jill Smith
　　　　　John Davies
　　　　　Barbara Forsdyke
　　　　　Julie McKenna (Secretary)

1 Apologies for absence were received from Mike Denton.

2 The minutes of the last meeting held on 22 September 1994 were accepted as a true record.

3 Matters Arising

　3.1　J Fisher has now obtained quotes from local kitchen companies and recommends that Kitchen Pride be given the job. They will commence work within the month.

4 Ordinary Business

　4.1　J Smith reported on the Barn Dance – ticket sales were disappointing, only 80 tickets being sold. However, those who attended had a most enjoyable evening and many expressed an interest in repeating this event next year. J Davies presented the Financial Statement for the evening. The reasons for the poor attendance were discussed and action decided upon to try to increase attendance at future social events.

　4.2　J Fisher has now acted on the committee's recommendation and booked the Murder Mystery Evening to take place on February 17th. 200 tickets will need to be sold to make a reasonable profit on the evening.

　4.3　J McKenna reported that all places for the Pantomine were now filled.

5 Any Other Business

　5.1　J Fisher raised the need for help from the rest of the committee with promoting events.

6 Date of Next Meeting

Thursday 26 January 1995 at 7.45 pm.

Financial Statement – Barn Dance

Expenditure

Printing tickets	10.00
Cost of venue	70.00
Caterers fees	240.00
Decorations for hall	20.00
Miscellaneous (Table covers etc.)	35.00
Band	150.00

Income

Ticket sales	480.00
Bar profit	110.00
Raffle profit	100.00

Outcomes	Action points
Kitchen work to commence	J Fisher to instruct Kitchen Pride to commence work
Sale of tickets for Murder Mystery Event	J Fisher to coordinate
Need for help with promotion of events	Committee

Task 4.26

Answer the following questions:

1 Compare the objectives of the event with the outcomes (all the information you need has been provided). Was the event a success?

2 How much were the tickets for the Barn Dance?

3 What was the profit made by the event?

4 Suggest a method that you could use to confirm that those who attended the Barn Dance did in fact have a good time.

5 Suggest reasons why ticket sales may have been disappointing.

6 Support was requested from the rest of the committee. Who asked for the support and what type of help was needed? How could other members of the committee help?

7 Suggest ways in which the target numbers for the Murder Mystery Evening may be achieved.

Element 4.3, PC1, 2, 3, 4, 5 and 6

After the disappointing response to the Barn Dance the committee has decided to review recent events undertaken to try to determine which were the most successful events in order to recapture this success in future events. Table 4.6 shows recent event attendance figures and cost of the ticket.

Table 4.6

Event	Target nos	Attending	Cost	Profit
French Meal	60	60	5.00	400
Quiz Night	80	40	1.50	60
Family Barbeque	100	200	3.50	300
Barn Dance	100	80	6.00	165

Task 4.27

Draw a graph to show actual numbers at each event compared with target numbers.

Using the figures above, suggest what type of events should be increased in the next year's social programme. Give reasons for your answer.
Element 4.3, PC1 and 6

In addition to reporting on the overall event, each individual should review and report back on their particular role within the event – including problems they encountered. It can be beneficial for the committee to offer their opinions on individual roles. However, it must be stressed that this should not be used as an opportunity to undermine other colleagues. Criticism should be encouraged, but it should be constructive with suggestions made on what an individual could do to improve their contribution. It is very easy to find fault, but not as easy to suggest ways to remedy these faults!

Once the event has been reviewed, problems that have arisen could be acted on through a staff development programme. This may be organized either within the organization itself or staff could be sent elsewhere to attend courses.

Case study

A local Amateur Dramatic Society has just finished a production of *A Midsummer Night's Dream*. When the group met to review this event two key areas were identified which had caused problems: make-up and stage lighting. They therefore decided that extra help was needed for people working in these areas. It was also suggested that in addition to the regular make-up team a few junior members should be encouraged to receive training in this skill to plan for future development. The action that the group took was to use some of the Society's funds to purchase a video on make-up and to organize a professional make-up artist to hold a teach-in with the make-up team. The development from this was that the make-up team felt that using their skills only for performances meant that they became rusty. Therefore it was decided that once a month make-up would be worn in rehearsal. This resulted in some very unusual and professional make-ups!

Task 4.28

Describe what effect this staff development may have on the make-up team. What difference might this make to future productions?
Element 4.3, PC6

The Lighting Manager for the Society was very fortunate. They wrote to the local theatre and explained the problem they had experienced. The Lighting Manager was invited to work with the lighting engineers at the theatre during their next production. He learned an amazing amount and was eager to put all this knowledge into practice.

Task 4.29

Suggest what course of action the Lighting Manager of the Amateur Dramatic Society should now take.
Element 4.3, PC6

As has been demonstrated in other sections of the book, the nature of the event will dictate organizational features. Evaluation is no exception to this. In considering events, small local events have been used to illustrate points made as these are the type of events that we are most familiar with and the ones that we are most likely to be involved in organizing. As has also been stated, evaluation should be closely linked to the purpose of the event. If the event is used to promote a venue, for example a theme park, repeat attendances would have to be closely monitored.

Organizing an event, if done well, can be a most enjoyable experience. The team spirit and togetherness that can be built up can lead to long-lasting friendships and may form the basis of frequent reminiscences, often revolving around the disasters or the humorous incidents that occurred. Most importantly, taking part in an event gives you a great feeling of satisfaction and achievement and can often be just the beginning. Many people who contribute to an event finish the evaluation process with:

'When is the next one?'

• Assignment 4.3 •

1 Hold a committee meeting to evaluate the event that you have undertaken. Produce accurate minutes using a recognized format.
2 Design an evaluation form that could be used to receive feedback from a variety of different sources.
3 Produce a report on the outcome of the event and put forward recommendations for future events.

INDEX

Related Reading......